Madley Church

THE OLD PARISH CHURCHES

OF HEREFORDSHIRE

Mike Salter

FOLLY PUBLICATIONS

ACKNOWLEDGEMENTS

The photographs and measured drawings in this book are the product of the author's fieldwork between 1971 and 1989. Old postcards, prints and brass rubbings are reproduced from originals in the author's collection. Thanks are due to Liz Pearce, John Lowe, Jo Wilkinson, Dennis Salter and Max Barfield for help with transport across Herefordshire and Worcestershire sometime during the last ten years.

ABOUT THIS BOOK

This book is a much extended and revised new edition of a book originally published in February 1990. As with the other books about churches in this series (see the full list inside the back cover) it concentrates on the period before the Industrial Revolution of the late 18th century. Most furnishings and monuments after 1770 are not mentioned, but additions and alterations to the fabric usually are, although in less detail. Churches founded after 1770 are not mentioned in the gazetteer, nor do they appear on the map. They are, however, listed towards the back of the book.

The book is inevitably very much a catalogue of dates and names, etc. It is intended as a field guide and for reference rather than to be read from cover to cover. Occasionally there is a comment about the setting of a church but on the whole little is said about their position or atmosphere. The amount of material given for a particular church in this book is not always a true indication of how interesting or attractive the building may be. Notable features of a church or the surrounding graveyard may lie outside the scope of this book as defined above. Visit them and judge for yourself. The gazetteer features Ordnance Survey grid references (these are the two letters and six digits which appear after each place-name and dedication) and the book is intended to be used in conjunction with O.S. 1:50,000 scale maps.

Plans redrawn from originals in the author's field notes are reproduced to a common scale of 1:400. The buildings were measured in metres and only metric scales are given. A system of hatching common to all the plans is used to denote the different periods of work. The plans should be treated with care and cross-referenced with the text since there are some things difficult to convey on small scale drawings (e.g. stones of one period being reset or reused in a later period). In some cases walling is shown as of a specific century but is in fact difficult to date.

ABOUT THE AUTHOR

Mike Salter is 44 and has been a professional writer since he went on the Government Enterprise Allowance Scheme for unemployed people in 1988. He is particularly interested in the planning and layout of medieval buildings and has a huge collection of plans of churches and castles he has measured during tours (mostly by bicycle and motorcycle) of England, Ireland, Scotland and Wales since 1968. Wolverhampton born and bred, Mike now lives in an old cottage beside the Malvern Hills. His other interests include model railways, board games, folk music, morris dancing, hill walking, and he plays a variety of percussion instruments.

ISBN 1 871731 32 1

Lugwardine Church

CONTENTS

Inside the front cover is a map of churches in the gazetteer.

INTRODUCTION

The district which from the early 11th century until 1974 formed the county of Herefordshire was converted to Christianity in the 7th century. It is likely that the county contained about fifty churches at the time of the Norman Conquest and certainly all those churches with dedications to obscure Celtic saints are early foundations. Some of these early churches may have been constructed of wood and those that were of stone have been rebuilt over the centuries. Thus the only relics of them are loose or reset carved stones at Llanveynoe, Munsley, Cradley, and Acton Beauchamp, plus the NE corner of the nave at Kilpeck with typically Saxon alternate long and short quoins or corner stones.

The boom in the construction of new parish churches of stone did not begin until the 1130s. Work likely to be of the period 1070-1130 appears only in about ten Herefordshire parish churches. Herringbone masonry with stone courses alternately sloping at 45 degrees to vertical appears in the naves at Wigmore, Letton, Munsley, Hatfield, and Edvin Loach, whilst the nave at Bredwardine has early-looking doorways. These naves all had the principal entrance on the south side but sometimes there was a second doorway opposite in the north wall. Small round headed windows set in embrasures with wide internal splays and having glass or shutters flush with the outside wall-face gave only minimal light. In the east wall would be a round arch opening into a small altar chamber called the chancel. Some chancels were square from the start but others were apsed until altered later, as at Bredwardine. More spacious chancels able to accommodate choirs were a later development as far as most ordinary parish churches were concerned. Hereford Cathedral and the priory church at Leominster were alone in possessing side aisles in this early period with large round piers supporting plain round arches.

Bredwardine Church

Ledbury

Peterchurch

Kilpeck

Yatton

Norman Doorways in Herefordshire

Castle Frome Church

Half of the churches described in the gazetteer have a mid or late 12th century nave or chancel, or both, which still survive, even if usually in a much altered state. Other churches retain from this period fonts, reset doorways and windows, and other loose fragments. Almost all the churches which existed in Herefordshire before the 19th century had been established by the year 1200. The county has remained mostly pastoral with little population growth in many of the villages. This helps to explain the high proportion of Norman work still remaining in the parish churches. Many English parish churches were enlarged in the later medieval period by the addition of aisles, but two thirds of the churches described in this book still have unaisled naves, and only a ninth of the churches have aisles on both north and south sides of the nave. The later centuries saw the provision of larger new windows, new roofs, the insertion of a wealth of furnishings and memorials, and walls built of easily-crumbling sandstone or shale were replaced as necessary, but the enlargement of the space needed to contain the congregation of a church was not often embarked upon in Herefordshire.

Parish churches of the period 1130-80 follow the same pattern as the earliest Norman churches. Kilpeck and Moccas are almost unaltered examples of three-celled churches, with a square chancel set between a nave and an apse. Peterchurch has four cells, a rarity, the extra compartment lying between the nave and chancel being the base of a former tower. No other churches have surviving apses but traces of them have been found at Tarrington and Mathon. Fownhope has a central tower still in a fairly complete state, and transepts remains of cruciform churches with central towers at Bromyard and Madley.

Herefordshire is particularly noted for architectural sculpture of this period, especially the work of a master craftsman and his followers who are referred to by modern experts as The Herefordshire School. The earliest work by the master appears at Shobdon in c1135-45 in three arches now reset in a folly on a hill above the present church. In the 1140s the master was at work on the south doorway at Kilpeck, and c1150 he or close associates produced the tympana remaining at Brinsop, Fownhope, Leominster, Stretton Sugwas, and the hospital of St Giles at Hereford. The chancel arch at Kilpeck is also by a member of this workshop (it does not appear to be by the master), and there are slightly later fonts in a similar style at Castle Frome and Eardisley. These examples show sculpture of great intensity with long narrow figures and beasts with long claws. It was inspired by Anglo-Saxon and Viking sculpture plus contemporary work in Northern Italy, Western France, and at Reading Abbey, the mother house of the priory at Leominster. So the workshop probably originated with craftsmen assembled at Leominster in the late 1120s to work upon parts of the priory church there which no longer survive.

Apart from the sculptural work just noted much of the mid 12th century work is plain and massive. By the 1170s the style becomes lighter and decoration is the norm. From the 1190s this round arched Romanesque style gradually gives way to the early Gothic style using the pointed arch, known in England as the Early English style. Gradually, piers were made more slender, windows become larger and the zig-zag or chevron motif first used sparingly just in the vertical plane in the 1120s becomes common in the 1170, both in the vertical and horizontal planes, and with other motifs. Ledbury has a long chancel of c1175-85 with typical clasping buttresses at the east corners and two bays of arches for side chapels, plus a fine nave west doorway of c1200. Bosbury church has been little altered since it was rebuilt with a fully aisled nave in the 1190s. Holmer has one large chamber serving as both nave and chancel, which is quite a common pattern in Wales and the adjoining parts of England. In c1180-1200 towers were added at Almeley, Bridge Sollers, Cradley, Dilwyn, Hampton Bishop, Wellington and Westhide. In the same period aisles were added at a dozen churches. The arcades of this period are more likely to survive than the aisle outer walls because the latter tended to need rebuilding later on either because they were decayed or more width was required, as at Bromyard, Upton Bishop and Weston-under-Penyard. Of a church built by the Knights' Templar at Garway in the 1190s the chancel arch and parts of the footings of the rare circular nave still remain.

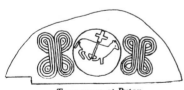

Tympanum at Byton

Tympanum at Fownhope

Doorway at Bromyard

Coddington Church

Belfry at Pembridge

Apart from the frequent insertion of new doorways and windows in older walls, a third of Herefordshire's medieval churches have structural work of the 13th century. A common pattern was for the chancel to be enlarged and then a few years later a west tower would be added to the original Norman nave. A fifth of the medieval churches in the county have a 13th century tower, a high proportion considering that half the churches have no proper tower, just a bellcote or timber belfry perched above the west gable of the nave. Prior to the 1270s chancels are plain and simple with three lancet windows in the east wall, and others in the side walls, as at Kington. The towers are equally plain and tend to be on the short side. The towers of c1200-40 at Bosbury, Garway, Kington and Ledbury, plus those of c1260 and c1300 respectively at Ewyas Harold and Richard's Castle are massive structures which may have had additional military functions. All of them, plus the tower of c1230 at Holmer with a later timber top, are or were detached. In the whole of England and Wales there are only about 40 detached medieval belfries and Herefordshire has no less than seven which are detached as they now stand. Several other towers, such as those in the two churches at Hereford, stand on one side of the nave rather than in the usual position at the west end. There are no surviving central towers of this period apart from one at Mordiford which was reduced to the height of the chancel c1812. Madley has a fine west tower which is embraced by aisles running the full length of what were then the nave and chancel. The porch at Clodock is a unusually early example of such an adjunct to a parish church, and there is 13th century work of note also remaining at Dilwyn, Much Marcle and Walford-on-Wye.

Interior of Bosbury Church

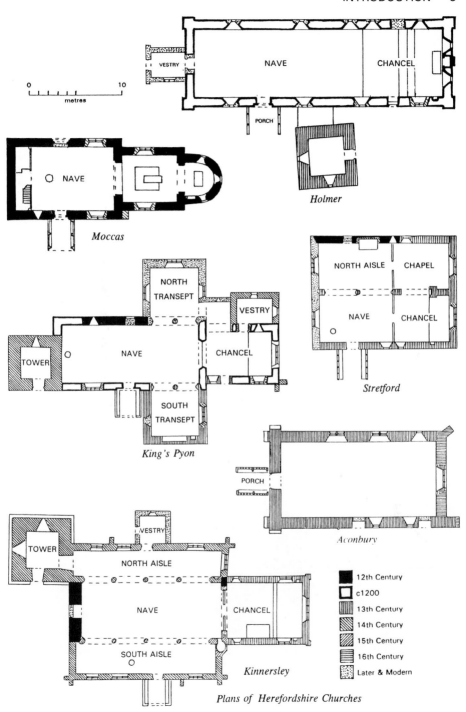

Plans of Herefordshire Churches

Stretton Grandison Church

Towards the end of the 13th century the simple Early English style developed into the more florid and showy style known in England as Decorated. There is much work of the period 1290-1350 to be seen in the churches although by the 1320s it was increasingly a matter of completing, altering, extending or repairing older structures rather than erecting new ones. There are many chancels of c1290-1320 and two dozen 14th century towers to add to those already built or begun by c1300. Spires are quite common in Herefordshire. Of those built of stone that at Withington may be as early as the 1290s but the other notable examples at Goodrich, Hereford, Llangarron, Peterchurch, Ross-on-Wye, Sellack, Stoke Edith, Stretton Grandison, and Weobley are all 14th century. Some of these churches have other major portions of that period. The tower at Weobley was originally detached, and at Yarpole and Pembridge are low timber-framed detached belfries. Of c1310-20 are the wide outer south aisle at Leominster and the north chapel at Ledbury with huge four-light windows studded with ballflowers, the apsed chancels at Madley and Marden, and almost all of the churches at Ashperton and Kingsland. The latter has shallow transepts, and indeed most of the transepts remaining in Herefordshire are of this period, as at Bodenham, Lyonshall, Mansell Gamage, Pembridge, Richard's Castle and Weobley. At Leintwardine the considerable 14th century parts include a large north chapel and a lofty SW porch-tower. The Decorated style in a more modest form is seen in the small churches of Huntingdon, Pencoyd, and Vowchurch.

Dilwyn Church

Bosbury, c1200-20

Ewyas Harold, c1260

Weobley, 14th century   *Peterstow, 15th century*   *St Weonards, c1520*

Five Herefordshire Church Towers

The late medieval building boom responsible for so much work in parish churches elsewhere in England made little impression on those of Herefordshire. There are about a dozen stone towers, some timber belfries, a number of porches both of stone and wood, a few inserted windows and much internal woodwork including roofs, but no complete churches and hardly any new churches, or transepts or chantry chapels. The towers all stand at the west end except for that at Much Marcle. The tower at Linton and the chapels at Bosbury, King's Caple and Sellack have stone vaulted ceilings. The church at St Weonards with an early 16th century tower and north aisle is the only one to have more work of this period (1400-1540) than of any other era.

Rotherwas chapel was rebuilt in the 1580s but contains too much work of earlier and later periods to be of importance. Four churches have unimportant towers of the period 1530-1600. In the early 17th century the only work of note was the restoration of the eastern part of the former abbey church of Dore. A new tower was added but the furnishings are of greater importance. Brampton Bryan church was wrecked by the Royalists during the Civil War and in the 1650s was mostly rebuilt as a wide single chamber covered with a hammerbeam roof. Of greater interest are the nave and chancel of 1679 at Monnington-on-Wye, and the tower, nave, and south transept of 1693 at How Caple.

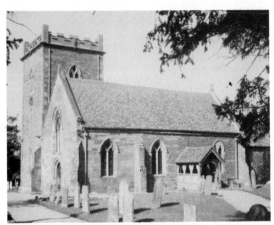

Kingstone Church

Interior of Bosbury Church

Much Cowarne Church

Interior of Welsh Newton Church

Tyberton Church

When Norton Canon church was rebuilt in brick in 1718 the old windows and their glass were carefully preserved. Alterations have spoiled the original character of the churches built at Tyberton in 1719, and Preston Wynne in 1727. The new church of 1740 at Whitney is not of much interest but work of the same period at Stoke Edith is memorable for the huge columns inside, not dividing off aisles, for none of these churches are aisled, but the east and west ends. By far the best church of this period is at Shobdon, as rebuilt in the Gothick style in the 1750s with ogival arches over the windows and a full set of matching furnishings. Several older churches have 18th century towers as at Eardisland and Eardisley, but none of these or any other additions of this period are of much importance. There is only one late 18th century church in Herefordshire and the 19th century buildings lie outside the scope of this book. Most of the medieval churches were repaired or rebuilding during that period, no less than ten being enlarged by adding a north aisle, and in one case a south aisle was added as well. Several towers were rebuilt and windows frequently renewed.

The earliest and simplest form of church roof was the trussed rafter type, the framing of which usually looks seven sided from below. Herefordshire examples are difficult to date and the only specimen for which a date is known is that at Longtown, erected as late as 1640. From the 14th century onwards there are many roofs with arched braces up to collar-beams with or without tie-beams below, king-posts, or raking struts forming trefoils or quatrefoils above, and tiers of wind braces also forming trefoils and quatrefoils. Coved roofs with wooden bosses are rare in Herefordshire, but there is an example at Kenderchurch. Hammerbeam roofs are also uncommon but occur at Hereford All Saints, 15th century, Holmer, c1500, Rotherwas, 1589, and Brampton Bryan, 1656.

Llanwarne Church

Doorways and masonry styles can help to date the different parts of old churches but usually the shape and style of the windows is the best evidence. However it should be remembered that windows may be later insertions in older walling or older openings reset. During the 12th century windows gradually increased in size from the tiny round headed openings of the Saxon and Norman periods to the lancet windows with pointed heads which appear in the 1190s at Bosbury and Holmer. Plain Norman windows appear in dozens of Herefordshire churches. More ornate windows like those with nook-shafts and roll-moulded surrounds at Kilpeck are rare. Windows with two narrow lights under an outer arch occur in the tower bell chambers at Eaton Bishop and Fownhope.

Large lancets with and without nook-shafts occur at Abbey Dore as early as c1200-20 and in many early to mid 13th century chancels such as those of Kington, Upton Bishop and Weston-under-Penyard. The usual arrangement is a widely spaced group of three in the east wall and evenly spaced single ones along the side walls. The tower at Madley has pairs and triplets of lancets more closely grouped. Probably of the 1260s are the trefoil-headed lights in pairs at Bridge Sollars, and the three lights under an outer arch in the tower bell-stage at Ewyas Harold. Below the latter is a two-light window with the space between the heads pierced by a lozenge. By widening the lights and making the subdividing mullions more delicate the Y-tracery typical of c1300 is produced. Intersecting tracery, as at Much Marcle, is the variant with three or more lights. Sometimes the arch heads and lozenges of this type of tracery have cusps. Geometrical tracery of the 1290s appears in the north aisle west window at Ledbury.

A style which was peculiar to Herefordshire in c1295-1325 is where there are three lights with the mullions rising straight up to the arch-head with sharply pointed heads only to the lights on either side, as at Much Marcle and Vowchurch. There are cinquefoiled circles in windows of c1310-20 at Marden and Leominster, the latter studded with ballflowers, but the curvilinear petal-like forms of the Decorated style in other parts of England are hardly found at all in Herefordshire. A common design of c1320-50 is reticulation or net-like tracery utilising the newly adopted ogival arch, as at Almeley, Llanwarne and Madley. Examples at Hampton Bishop and Kinnersley with longer reticulation units are of c1360-1400.

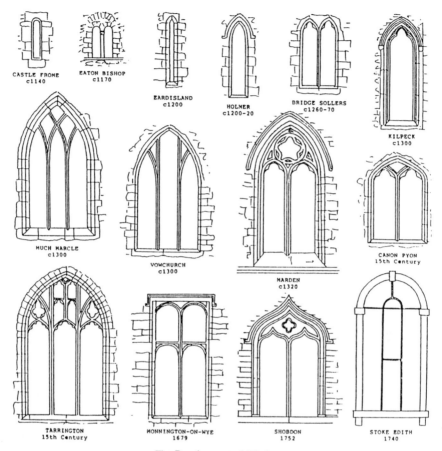

The Development of Windows

The motif already described of uninterupted mullions rising straight up to the main arch, but now often with minor subdivisions of the lights, is the hallmark of the Perpendicular style in vogue from the late 14th century until the 1530s. Leominster Priory has a huge west window of this type with two of the many mullions taking the form of stepped buttresses. More typical is the west window at Richard's Castle, but other late medieval windows in Herefordshire call for little comment. The four-centred arch is used sometimes, as at Tarrington and in the chapel of c1510 at Bosbury. Square-headed two light windows with the lights simply cusped or even uncusped are common.

Unaltered windows of the late 16th, 17th, and 18th centuries are rare in Herefordshire parish churches. Monnington-on-Wye of 1769 has mullion-and-transom windows with segmental arches over all the lights. The simple round arch is used in the 18th century as at Stoke Edith. More exiting is the return of the ogival form for the main arch and the heads of the lights at Shobdon in the 1750s. The Victorians experimented with all the older styles and examples of that period occur frequently in the medieval churches. Some reproduce what was there before, others ignore the type of predecessors, and others are completely new openings.

Norman fonts are numerous in Herefordshire. Two dozen are noted as of interest in the gazetteer and there are many more simple plain tubs which cannot be closely dated. Apart from those of the 1150s by the Herefordshire School at Castle From and Eardisley there are others of note at How Caple and Michaelchurch. There are several fonts from each of the later medieval periods and a slightly larger group of the 17th century. Lea has an Italian stoup of c1200 in use as a font. At Burghill a Norman font now serves as the base for a 13th century lead bowl with foliage. The 13th century font at Hope-under-Dinmore has arcading with figures, whilst the 14th century font at Weobley has panels on blank traceried windows. The badges and panelling at Fownhope are typically late medieval. Aston Ingram has a lead bowl dated 1689 and Credenhill a fluted bowl dated 1667.

In the later medieval period it became customary for the chancel of a church to be divided off from the nave by a screen with a Rood or image of the crucifixion set over it. Sometimes the screen bore a loft used by musicians and the performers of religious plays, these being an important means of conveying God's message in an era when services were conducted in Latin, which only a few of the congregation could understand. Over screens divided off side chapels and transepts. Some screens were ripped out during the Reformation of the mid 16th century when idols were banned and the priest's activities in the chancel were supposed to be more open to view, but simple screens without images or lofts were still being provided in the 17th century, as at Abbey Dore. The 19th century restorations saw many more screens removed, replaced or cut down. Stairs which gave access to the former lofts often remain, as at Little Hereford and Pembridge. Two dozen churches in Herefordshire have old screens or the remains of them. Welsh Newton has a very rare 14th century stone screen. Others of wood dating from c1400-1540 can be seem at Aymestry, Bosbury, Burghill and St Margarets.

Font at Orleton

Font at Burghill

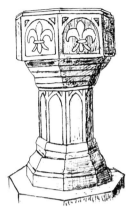

Font at Fownhope

Rood loft at St Margarets

*Doorway at
Much Marcle*

Interior of Shobdon Church

Medieval pulpits are rare as sermons only became fashionable in the 16th century. Weobley has fragments of a 14th century stone pulpit and there are others of the 15th century and c1530 of wood at Stretton Grandison and Wigmore. A few pulpits may be Elizabethan but by far the biggest group apart from Victorian ones, are those of c1610-40. Some have classical motifs such as arcading and pilasters, etc. A few medieval doors survive and there are instances of old ironwork being reused on later doors. A Norman doorknocker remains at Dormington. Some churches have communion rails around the altar table dating from the 16th, 17th or 18th centuries. Late medieval tiles with heraldic designs survive in several places. There is medieval glass in about twenty churches, but single figures and fragments are more common than complete windows. Madley has 13th century medallions and part of a 14th century Tree of Jesse. Other 14th century glass remains at Credenhill, Dilwyn and Eaton Bishop. At Leintwardine and Hampton Bishop are remains of stone medieval reredoses. Stalls fitted with miserichords (hinged seat to support the behinds of standing choristers) remain at Canon Pyon, Holme Lacy, Leintwardine at St Peter's at Hereford. Originally each church possessed a lockable chest in which plate was kept. Those at Garway, Kingstone and Orleton are carved out of single trunks.

Tomb at Croft

Tomb chest at Bridstow

Coffin lid at Woolhope

Tomb at Eye

There are four dozen effigies, four engraved brasses, five incised slabs inlaid with pitch, and three indents once filled with some sort of composition surviving from before 1540 in the parish churches of Herefordshire. Two thirds, an unusually high proportion, are of the 13th and 14th centuries. Also of that period are the coffin lids with floriated crosses on them at about a dozen churches, plus the plain shrine-like tomb-chests at Bridstow and Goodrich. Sollars Hope has an incised slab of as early as c1225. There are rare oak effigies of c1300 and c1370 at Clifford and Much Marcle. The earliest effigies of stone are the ladies at Woolhope and Welsh Bicknor, and the knights at Abbey Dore, all late 13th century. There are notable later effigies at Clehonger, Croft, Kington, Ledbury, Much Marcle, Pembridge, Ross-on-Wye and Weobley. The latter also has the best brass, depicting a knight that died in 1483. Edvin Loach has four notable monuments of the period 1275-1340.

Ross-on-Wye   *17th century tomb at Castle Frome Church*

Over 70 monuments of the period 1540-1700 survive in addition to many plain inscriptions which are not noted in the gazetteer. The series of tomb chests with recumbent effigies on the lid continues until the Civil War period, as at Holme Lacy, 1571, Madley, 1575, Ross-on-Wye, 1635, and Much Marcle, 1650. Some effigies are set against a round arch as in those of the 1570s at Bosbury. Kneeling couples set under arches are common, as at Much Dewchurch, 1625, and those of the 1630s at Kinnersley and Ledbury. At Bacton is a rustic monument showing one of Queen Elizebeth's maids-of-honour kneeling beside her. The few brasses of this period also usually show figures kneeling towards each other or an altar, as at Lugwardine, 1622. The 17th century clerics at Ledbury, Lugwardine and Foy are shown as frontal demi-figures, usually holding books. At Monnington in 1667 a mere bust suffices, but two colonels of the Civil War are commemorated by full size statues at Ross-on-Wye and Weobley.

Tablet at Castle Frome Church

The emphasis on effigies decreased during the 17th century and eventually mural tablets with lengthy inscriptions became normal. Sometimes these have architectural surrounds, urns, cherubs, the symbols of death or a profession, and other adornments. A dozen tablets of 1654 to 1714 have the twisted columns often used in the Baroque architectural style. Cast-iron ledger stones with lettering only appear from 1619 to 1678 at Burrington, and also at Brilley.

GAZETTEER OF OLD CHURCHES IN HEREFORDSHIRE

ABBEY DORE   *St Mary*   SO 387304

Dore Abbey was a Cistercian monastery founded in 1147. A large new cruciform church 75m long was built c1175-90. It originally had a two bay chancel flanked by pairs of one bay chapels opening off the transepts but the innermost chapels were absorbed into aisles of a longer chancel with an eastern ambulatory built c1200-20. Cistercian churches rarely saw further use after the Dissolution but here in the 1630s Lord Scudamore had a new west wall built to close off the decayed eastern parts for parochial use. They were then re-roofed by John Abel and a tower was erected above the south chancel aisle. The nave and cloistral buildings were abandoned and little now remains of any of them. The font, the screen, the stalls, benches, pulpit and tester, the west gallery, communion rail and some stained glass all date from the 1630s. There are also older fragments of glass, various sculptured stones from the abbey buildings, 13th century heraldic tiles, two damaged effigies of 13th century knights, and a tomb chest of John Hoskins, d1638.

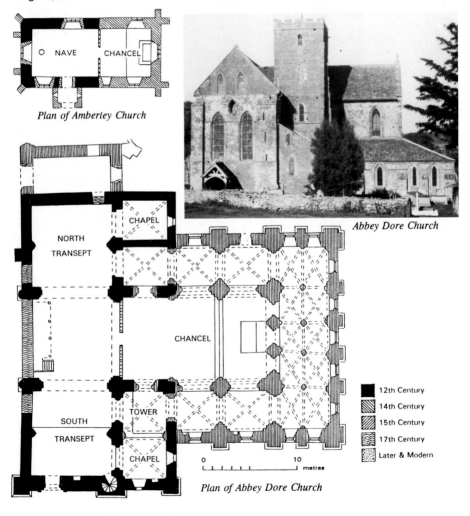

Plan of Amberley Church

Abbey Dore Church

NAVE   CHANCEL

NORTH TRANSEPT

CHAPEL

CHANCEL

SOUTH TRANSEPT

TOWER

CHAPEL

- ■ 12th Century
- ▨ 14th Century
- ▧ 15th Century
- ▦ 17th Century
- ▨ Later & Modern

0   10
metres

Plan of Abbey Dore Church

Aconbury Church

ACONBURY   *St John the Baptist*   SO 517336

A convent of sisters of the order of St John of Jerusalem founded here in the 1230s by Margaret, wife of William de Lacy, was shortly afterwards transferred to Augustinian canonesses. They built the present single chamber in the late 13th century. It has several original windows, one on the west having three quatrefoils above three trefoil-headed lancets. Below it is a doorway with a 15th century timber porch. The two blocked south doorways once led to the claustral buildings and a tiny chamber high up in the SW corner was reached from the dormitory. The east end was shortened in the 16th century using older materials. At this end there is now the Chandos family burial vault of the late 17th or early century. In a tomb recess of c1300 inside is a coffin lid with an incised floriated cross and an inscription of Lombardic letters to Maud de Gerney, wife of Roger Clifford. See plan on page 9.

ACTON BEAUCHAMP   *St Giles*   SO 680504

The short west tower with a pyramidal roof is probably medieval. It has a south doorway with a lintel formed from a portion of a finely carved 9th century cross-shaft with various creatures. The nave and chancel were rebuilt in 1819 except for the late 12th century south doorway with nook-shafts and a roll-moulded arch.

ALLENSMORE   *St Andrew*   SO 467358

From the Late Norman south doorway has come the 12th century capital now lying on top of the shaft of the churchyard cross. The nave and chancel are otherwise of c1280-1300 and have several windows of that period. The east window with reticulated tracery and fragments of original glass must be of c1330, and the west tower, north doorway, and one north window are 15th century. There is an incised cross slab in the nave and in the chancel is a large late 14th century incised slab to Sir Andrew Herle and his wife Joan, plus a tablet and scrolls to Richard Crumor, d1702. There is also a Jacobean pulpit.

Almeley Church

ALMELEY   *St Mary*   SO 332516

The short west tower was begun c1200. The chancel dates from the end of the 13th century. It has a Geometrical style east window and a chancel arch supported on busts, with another bust at the apex. The tomb recess with an ogival top must be slightly later. The four bay aisles and the nave clerestory are early 14th century. The roof has a pretty ceilure' with painted Tudor roses above the rood screen. The rood staircase is 14th century. The tower arch screen is Jacobean.

AMBERLEY   *Dedication Unknown*   SO 546479

The nave masonry and the reset outer entrance of the porch are Norman. The porch itself, the double bellcote, and most of the other features are early 14th century. Inside the east wall is a castellated 15th century frame.

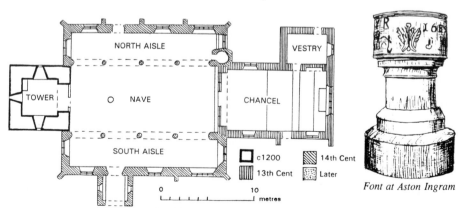

Plan of Almeley Church

Font at Aston Ingram

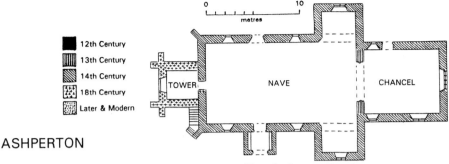

12th Century
13th Century
14th Century
18th Century
Later & Modern

TOWER NAVE CHANCEL

ASHPERTON

St Bartholomew SO 643415

Plan of Ashperton Church

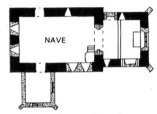

NAVE

The chancel, the wide aisleless nave and the small transepts are all early 14th century, built probably under patronage by William de Grandison, licensed in 1292 to embattle his house immediately to the west. Only the chancel arch seems to be earlier. The west tower is an addition or rebuilding of c1800. There is a tablet with columns and a segmental pediment to a 17th century member of the Wilson family.

Plan of Aston Church

ASTON *St Giles* SO 461718

The Norman nave has original north and south doorways but most of the windows have been renewed. The tympanum over the south doorway has a lamb with a cross in a circle held by the bull of St Luke and the eagle of St John, and an outer band with animals and foliage. The nave has a roof with tie-beams, queen-posts, collar-beams and wind braces. It probably dates from the 17th century.

ASTON INGRAM *St John the Baptist* SO 693236

The church was mostly rebuilt by Nicholson & Son in 1871 except for the south doorway and chancel arch of c1200, the 16th century west tower set within the nave, the lead font of 1689 with foliage and initials, and the two 13th century effigies lying on either side of the altar.

Ashperton Church

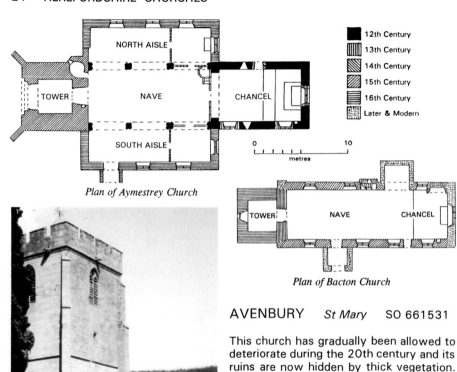

Plan of Aymestrey Church

■	12th Century
▦	13th Century
▨	14th Century
▧	15th Century
▤	16th Century
▦	Later & Modern

Plan of Bacton Church

Aymestrey Church

AVENBURY   *St Mary*   SO 661531

This church has gradually been allowed to deteriorate during the 20th century and its ruins are now hidden by thick vegetation. Little now remains of the nave, which once had a north aisle with a three bay arcade, but the late 12th century chancel and early 13th century tower still mostly survive.

AYLTON   SO 658377

The Norman nave has one original north window. The south doorway, the east extension which forms the chancel, and the screen are 14th century. The south porch of 1654 with balusters and the nave west wall were rebuilt later.

AYMESTREY   *St John the Baptist and St Alkmund*   SO 426651

The Norman chancel has two original north windows. The quatrefoil shaped arcade piers are also Norman. They are either reset or have been brought in from elsewhere and given new capitals and arches. One suggested source for them is Wigmore Abbey but the Norman nave there was aisleless and the piers are not likely to have come from the domestic buildings. The west tower and the aisles are late 15th century to early 16th century, the campaign culminating c1540 with the insertion of a fine rood screen with linenfold panelling on the dado and a coving with lierne ribs, plus the two parclose screens in the aisles. The pulpit is Jacobean and there is an incised alabaster slab to Sir John Lingen, d1506, and his wife, plus a large classical style tablet with Doric pilasters to Robert Weever, d1728.

BACTON   *St Faith*   SO 371324

The tower was rebuilt c1575 except for the 13th century arch towards the nave. The single bodied church is otherwise 15th century and retains a roodloft staircase on the north side. The east wall was rebuilt in 1894 although the window in it is original. The vestry and porch are also Victorian. The nave has a trussed rafter roof, and the chancel has a wagon roof with bosses. Both are 15th century. The stalls are late medieval, and there is a fine 17th century altar frontal. An interesting feature is a rustic monument to Blanche Parry, maid of honour to Elizabeth I. Blanche is shown kneeling beside the Queen. There is also a tablet to Alexander Stantar, d1620, with kneeling figures of him an his wife facing each other. Another tablet is to Rachel Hopton, d1663, wife of Lewis Thomas.

BALLINGHAM   *St Dubricius*   SO 576317

The nave has an early 13th century north lancet and a later 13th century north window whilst the south doorway and roof are 14th century. The west tower is late 14th century. The chancel and rib-vaulted south porch are 15th century. The pulpit is Jacobean and there is a black and white tablet to William Scudamore, d1649.

BARTESTREE   *St James*   SO 567409

The present church is of 1888 by Nicholson and Son. The former 15th century chapel of Old Longworth in the parish of Lugwardine, latterly in use as a barn, was transferred in 1869-70 to another site to serve a convent founded in 1863 under patronage of the Phillipps family, two of which have monuments within it. The chapel has an original collar beam roof and a medieval door with tracery in the porch.

BIRLEY   *St Peter*   SO 454534

The Norman nave has an original south doorway and early and late 13th century windows. The chancel is 13th century but the chancel arch is 14th century, with ballflowers, and heads on the shafts. The south chapel is late 14th century with a later roof and timber framed gable. The west tower was built c1200 and has round-headed lower windows but a pointed tower arch with early crocket capitals. The bell-stage projects slightly and has a pyramidal roof. The Norman font has saltire crosses, arches and a plait.

Bacton: Monument to Blanche Parry

BISHOP'S FROME   *St Mary*   SO 664484

The neo-Norman nave and north aisle are of 1861 and the chancel is of 1847. Only the chancel arch with chevron ornamentation and the south doorway with two orders of shafts with waterleaf capitals are real 12th century work. The west tower is 14th century, the screen is partly old, and there is a late 13th century effigy of a knight drawing his sword set in a later recess with ball-flowers. A painted monument to Margery de la Downes, d1598, has two kneeling figures and a skeleton below, along with many interesting inscriptions.

BISHOPSTONE   *St Lawrence*   SO 417438

There is a blocked Norman window in the nave south wall. The west windows also look Norman but the whole wall is 14th century, as are several other windows and the timber south porch which has been transferred here from Yazor old church. The transepts and chancel are 13th century. There are panels of foreign 16th and 17th century glass in a south window and in the north transept are recumbent effigies of John Berinton, d1614, and his wife.

BLAKEMERE   *St Leonard*   SO 362411

The church was rebuilt in 1877 and the internal facing is all of that period, but the south doorway and chancel arch are of c1200. The priest's doorway and a chancel north window also appear Late Norman, the chancel east wall has 13th century lancets, and there are several other later medieval windows. The Norman font has a rope moulding at the foot of the bowl. The pulpit is Jacobean.

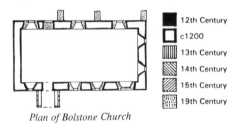

■ 12th Century
□ c1200
▦ 13th Century
▨ 14th Century
▧ 15th Century
▥ 19th Century

Plan of Bolstone Church

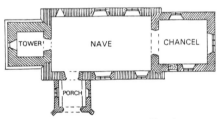

Plan of Ballingham Church

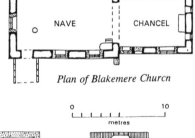

Plan of Blakemere Churcn

0 |___|___|___|___|___| 10
metres

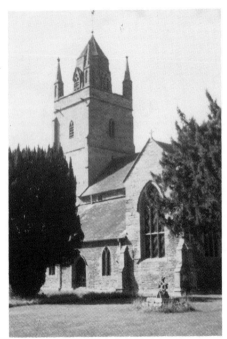

Bodenham Church

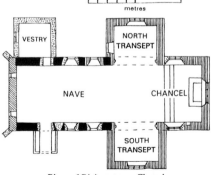

Plan of Bishopstone Church

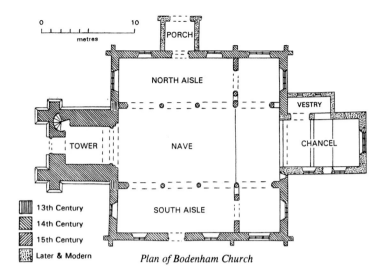

Plan of Bodenham Church

BODENHAM   *St Michael*   SO 530509

The west corners of a spacious 13th century nave survive. The wide aisles with four bay arcades, the porch, and big tower with angle buttresses are all 14th century. The doorways have ballflowers. The tower was given a pyramidal roof over the stump of an incomplete recessed spire. The chancel was also 14th century but has been rebuilt and shortened at the east end. The east bays of the aisles were made into transepts with tall end windows in the 15th century. The 16th century clerestory includes reset 14th century windows. There is also a 14th century female effigy with a child standing by her side.

BOLLINGHAM   *St Silas*   SO 302527

The 19th century rebuilding left only the original south walls and the roof with tie-beams, king-posts and collar-beams.

BOLSTONE   *Dedication Unknown*

SO 552327

Although mostly rebuilt in 1877 this little used chapel has rounded headed doorways and two east windows of c1200, plus two later south windows. The Jacobean octagonal font has fleur-de-lis, a thistle, and a flower on it.

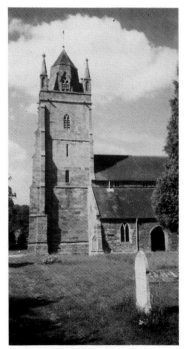

Bodenham Church

Bosbury Church

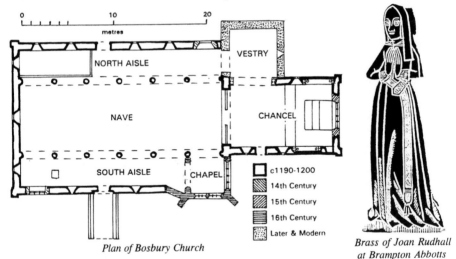

Plan of Bosbury Church

Brass of Joan Rudhall at Brampton Abbotts

BOSBURY   *Holy Trinity*   SO 695435

The aisled nave with six bay arcades and the chancel represent a substantial church of c1190-1200.There are clasping corner pilasters. Most of the lancet windows have pointed heads but the west window and doorways are round arched. The large detached tower some way to the south is 13th century. The eastern bay of the south aisle was rebuilt as a chapel c1510 by Thomas Morton, whose initials appear on the fan-vaulted ceiling. There is also a large 19th century north vestry. The font of c1200 stands on five columns. The screen is medieval, the pulpit and reader's desk contain 16th and 17th century woodwork, and the lectern is Jacobean. In the south aisle is a 14th century coffin lid with a foliated cross and two other crosses. In the chancel are monuments to John Harford, d1573, and Richard Harford, d1578, and his wife.

Brampton Abbotts Church

BRAMPTON ABBOTTS   *St Michael*   SO 602265

The nave and chancel are both Norman. The south doorway and chancel arch each have one order of shafts, although the arch of the latter is a 16th century rebuild. The nave roof is 14th century and the font is 15th century. There is a brass of Joan Rudhall, c1520. The figures of her husband John, d1507, and children are missing.

BRAMPTON BRYAN   *St Barnabas*   SO 370725

As rebuilt in 1656 for Sir Robert Harley after destruction before or during a Royalist attack on the adjacent castle in 1644, the church has a short but wide single chamber corresponding to the width of the medieval nave and north aisle. It is covered by a double hammer-beam roof. A blocked former tower arch of c1200 remains in the southern half of the west wall. The pulpit has 17th century panels. A 14th century effigy of a lady holding her heart in her hand lies in a recess with 14th and 15th century tiles in the south wall, and there is a large monument to Sir Robert's descendant, the 2nd Earl of Oxford, d1724.

BREDWARDINE   *St Andrew*   SO 335445

The Early Norman nave has four original windows, tufa quoins, and north and south doorways with large lintels carved with rosettes and strange looking deities. The space once occupied by an apse was later taken into the nave and this part has a 14th century south wall. Beyond is a new chancel of c1300 very irregularly laid out with a sharp incline to the north. The tower on the north side was added in 1790. There is a large plain Norman font. On either side of the altar are effigies of knights, one being a late 14th century member of the Baskerville family, whilst the other, mid 15th century, represents one of the Foulshurst family. There is also a cartouche of 1703 to Elizabeth, wife of Thomas Hodges.

BREINTON   *St Michael*   SO 474395

Only the west doorway of c1200, parts of three Norman west windows, a 14th century chancel window, and some of the masonry on the south side survived the rebuilding of 1866-70 by R.F.Kempson. Inside is a rustic painted tablet to Captain Rudhall Booth, d1685.

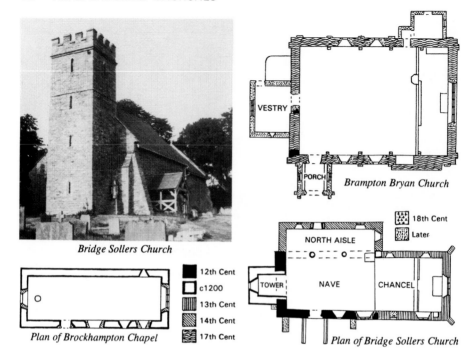

Brampton Bryan Church

Bridge Sollers Church

■ 18th Cent

▨ Later

Plan of Brockhampton Chapel

- 12th Cent
- c1200
- 13th Cent
- 14th Cent
- 17th Cent

NORTH AISLE

TOWER   NAVE   CHANCEL

Plan of Bridge Sollers Church

BRIDGE SOLLERS   *St Andrew*   SO 415426

The Norman nave has an original south window and a doorway with the outer arch carried on a head with two dragons emanating from the mouth and a dragon in profile. The two eastern bays of the arcade are of c1180 and the thin west tower is just a little later. The chancel is of c1300 and the aisle was rebuilt and extended in the 14th century, the third arch, pointed but unmoulded, being of that date.

BRIDSTOW   *St Bridget*   SO 585249

Only the Norman chancel arch with chevrons, the 13th century two bay arcade to a north chapel, and the late 14th century tower survived the rebuilding by Thomas Nicholson in 1862. A 13th century tomb chest with cusped on colonettes lies in a recess in the chancel. There is an old door in the south aisle.

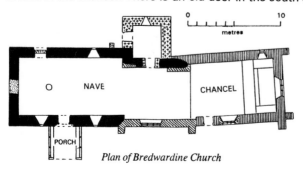

0 |_|_|_|_|_|_|_|_|_|_| 10
metres

NAVE   CHANCEL

PORCH

Plan of Bredwardine Church

Brobury Church

BRILLEY   *St Mary*

SO 260493

The thin west tower is of 1912, the chancel was rebuilt in 1890, and the nave windows have been renewed, but the transeptal north chapel is of c1300 and the roofs are old. That over the nave has tie-beams, one having cusped raking struts and a cusped collar. There are two cast-iron memorial slabs of 1669-70.

BRIMFIELD   *St Michael*

SO 526675

The Norman west tower has a 17th century timber-framed top stage. The nave and chancel were rebuilt in the 19th century.

Brimfield Church

BRINSOP   *St George*   SO 442448

The single chamber nave and chancel with a four bay arcade to a north aisle are mostly of c1300-50, but the chancel has some older walling. There are wall paintings of c1300 and c1330 showing the Annunciation and Visitation and the Crucifixion. There is a very fine tympanum of c1150-60 depicting St George plus other Norman sculptured fragments. There are two coffin lids with foliated crosses. The stoup is 15th century, there is an old screen and also a tablet William Dansey, d1708.

BROBURY   *St Mary Magdalene*   SO 345443

The chancel of c1300 with a reset later tomb recess and a 17th century roof now forms a private house, extended in the 1980s by building a metal framed octagonal tower on the site of the nave demolished in 1853.

BROCKHAMPTON-BY-BROMYARD   *Dedication Unknown*   SO 686560

West of Lower Brockhampton House is a ruined single chamber chapel with windows dating from c1200, the 13th century and the late 14th century. A new chapel designed by George Byfield was built c1798 near Brockhampton Park.

BROCKHAMPTON-BY-ROSS   *Holy Trinity*   SO 597317

The ruined old church by Brockhampton Court Hotel is probably 13th century. Two windows are 15th century and the west tower and south porch are late 16th century. The new church of All Saints designed by W.R.Lethaby to the NW is of 1901-2.

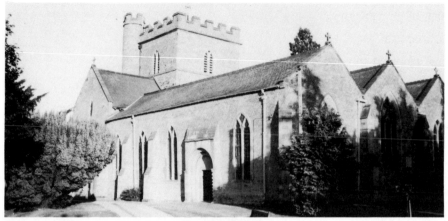

Bromyard Church

BROMYARD   *St Peter*   SO 656548

Of a cruciform Norman church there remains the masonry of the nave west wall, the transepts and the splendid reset north and south doorways with three orders of shafts, and lozenges, rosettes, and chevrons on the arches. A pointed arch was later cut into the tympanum of the south doorway. Aisles with five bay arcades were added on the south and north c1190 and c1210 respectively. The piers were heightened in 1805. In the early 14th century the crossing piers were renewed and a new tower raised above them, a long new chancel added, and the aisles widened to equal the projection of the transepts. The many tomb recesses both inside and out are also of that era whilst the north transept end window is slightly earlier. The buttresses, vestry, and the windows of the chancel, plus the western buttresses are Victorian. There is a Norman panel with a relief of St Peter above the south doorway. The font with chevrons, a tree of life and a running scroll motif is also Norman. The metal bushel of 1670 was once used as a legal measure.

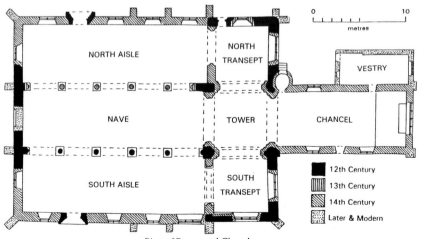

Plan of Bromyard Church

Burghill Church

BURGHILL   *St Mary*   SO 480445

There is a reset Norman doorway between the wide chancel and the 14th century vestry, and a Norman window lies nearby. Aisles were added to the nave c1200 but only the south aisle end walls, a north aisle end wall, and the west respond of the north arcade have survived the replacement of the five bay arcades in the early 13th and 14th centuries and a heavy restoration in 1880. The tower was rebuilt in 1812. The stem and the rim of the lead bowl of the font are of c1200, the pulpit is Jacobean, and there is a medieval screen with a coving deep enough to require support from a pair of Jacobean posts. The communion rail is late 17th century. On a tomb chest are recumbent effigies of Sir John Milbourne and his wife, c1440. A brass inscription and globe commemorate the traveller Robert Masters, d1619.

BURRINGTON   *St George*   SO 443721

The church was mostly rebuilt in the 1850s. Outside to the east are six cast-iron slabs dating from 1619-78. One is to Richard Knight, d1645. His family, noted iron-masters, probably produced the many similar slabs at Bridgnorth.

Brass to Robert Masters at Burghill

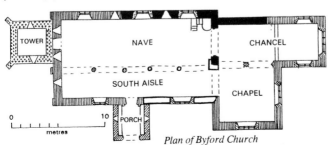

Plan of Byford Church

BYFORD   *St John the Baptist*   SO 397429

The eastern part of the nave, with one original north window, and the western part of the chancel formed the original Norman church. A three bay south aisle was added c1190. Two more bays to the west, a new south doorway and a square south chapel with a two bay arcade to the chancel were added in the 13th century. The chancel was doubled in length c1300. Of the 14th century are the windows and wall-painting of St Margaret in the south chapel and the south porch. The font dated 1638 has four badges upon it. The west tower was added in 1717. See page 33.

BYTON   *St Mary*   SO 371642

The hill-top church of 1859-60 has a Norman font with chevrons and against the south wall lies a Norman tympanum with the Lamb and Cross.

CALLOW   *St Mary*   SO 490344

In the church of 1830, altered in 1884, is a 14th century font.

CANON FROME   *St James*   SO 645435

The church lies beside Canon Frome Court. Except for the brick west tower of 1680 it was entirely rebuilt in 1860 by Bodley.

*Priest's Doorway
at Canon Pyon*

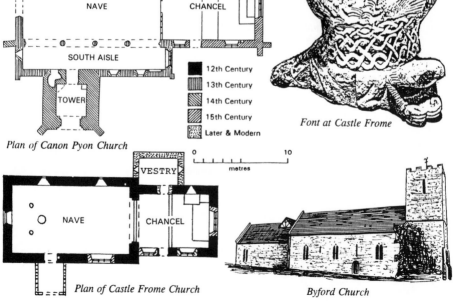

NORTH AISLE   CHAPEL

NAVE   CHANCEL

SOUTH AISLE

■ 12th Century
▥ 13th Century
▨ 14th Century
▧ 15th Century
▦ Later & Modern

TOWER

Plan of Canon Pyon Church

Font at Castle Frome

VESTRY

0   10
metres

NAVE   CHANCEL

Plan of Castle Frome Church

Byford Church

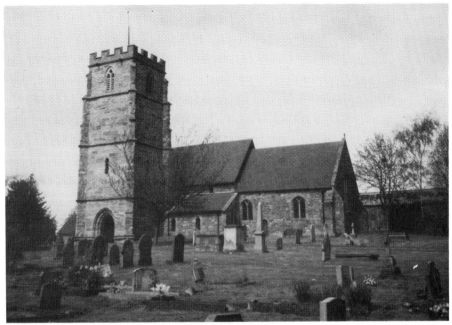

Canon Pyon Church

CANON PYON *St Lawrence* SO 450492

The wide nave and chancel are undivided except by an old screen. The dramatically leaning north and south arcades of the early and late 13th century respectively were originally both of four bays. An extra bay to serve a new north chapel was added in the 14th century when the aisle was widened and the original east repond reset. Most of the windows and the porch-tower on the south side are 14th century. The east window and the priest's doorway are 15th century. The tower helps to support the south arcade by means of flying buttresses. The 15th century font has a quatrefoil frieze and there are stalls with miserichords carved with various animals. The indents with the outlines of a man and woman of c1400 were filled with a sort of cement composition. There is a monument to George Sawyer, d1753.

CASTLE FROME *St Michael* SO 667459

This is basically a little altered Norman church with original windows on the northg and west sides. One south window is 14th century and two south windows, the east window, and the chancel ceilure with panels, diagonal ribs and bosses are 15th century. The pretty timber framed bell turret and south porch date from the sensitive restoration of 1878 by Martin Buckle. Inside is a particularly fine font of c1170 carved with the Baptism of Christ, the signs of the Evangelists, and two doves. The pulpit has some plain late 17th century panels whilst the stalls have Jacobean arches on the fronts. There are old tiles in the back of the piscina and a nave south window has some 15th century glass. Reset in a chancel window is a small bust of a knight holding what appears to be his heart. There is also a tomb chest with recumbent alabaster effigies of c1650, and a tablet to Frances Unett, d1656. See page 19.

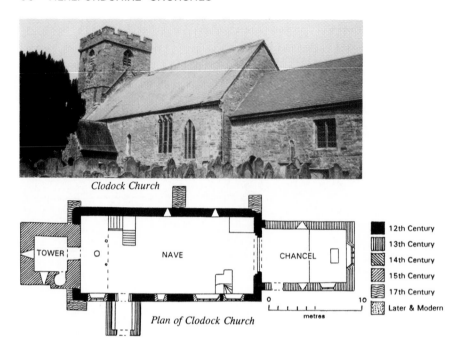

Clodock Church

Plan of Clodock Church

■	12th Century
⬚	13th Century
▨	14th Century
▨	15th Century
▨	17th Century
▨	Later & Modern

CLEHONGER   *All Saints*   SO 466378

Relics of the Norman church are the nave west window now looking into an early 13th century tower, the reset south doorway with a keeled roll moulding and colonettes with waterleaf capitals, and the stone with chevrons reused in the south wall of the chancel of c1300. The four bay arcade is mid 13th century whilst the aisle itself has windows with Y-tracery of c1300. Another window of that period is reset in the north chapel built by Sir Richard Pembrugge to serve a chantry he founded in 1341 to contain his very fine effigy. The smaller effigy of a lady may be his widow. Also in the chapel are brasses of Sir John Barre, d1483, and his wife, and there is part of 13th century foliated cross slab and a tablet to Herbert Aubrey, d1671, and his wife.

CLIFFORD   *St Mary*   SO 252450

The church lies in woods far from the village. The priest's doorway and the round arched recess in the chancel are Norman. Otherwise the chancel is early 13th century, the nave is late 13th century, the west tower is 18th century with older material, and the north aisle is of 1887. There is an oak effigy of c1300.

CLODOCK   *St Clodock*   SO 327275

The large nave has two Norman windows and a wide chancel arch of c1190. The chancel is 13th century and has one 16th century window. The east window and one in the nave are of c1300. The west tower and two south windows are 15th century. The porch looks c1200, but could be part of the extensive 17th century repairs. There are pews dated 1660, 1668, and 1701, a three decker pulpit and tester, stalls of 1657, a west gallery of c1715, and an inscribed 9th century tombstone.

Colwall Church

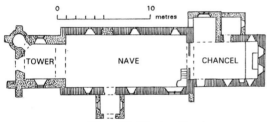

Plan of Coddington Church

Clehonger Church

CODDINGTON   *All Saints*   SO 718427

The round headed doorways suggest a date of c1200 but the nave and chancel both have several 13th century lancets, and a dedication of three altars in the church took place in 1231. The nave roof with collar-beams on arched braces forming two-centred arches could also be of the 13th century. The west tower with a broach spire was built in 1865 by Kempson, and the porch and vestry are also Victorian.

COLLINGTON   *St Mary*   SO 449601

A 13th century font with arches on colonettes lies in the church of 1856.

COLWALL   *St James*   SO 739423

The Late Norman south doorway has colonettes with trumpet scallop capitals. The south aisle with a five bay arcade is 13th century. Projecting south from the west end of the aisle is a tower begun in the 14th century but with a 15th century top. The nave has a fine old roof with collar-beams on arched braces and two tiers of wind braces. The existing chancel was built in 1865 by Woodyer, and the north aisle was added in 1880. The pulpit and tester are 17th century. In the north aisle is a 13th century tile showing one of the labours of the months, and in the south aisle is a brass depicting Elizabeth Harford, d1590.

Cradley Church

CRADLEY   *St James*   SO 736471

The tower arch suggests the large tower was built c1200, and the chancel and nave doorways are Late Norman. The latter has colonettes and a chevron pattern. The chancel was rebuilt in 1868, and the large nave was rebuilt and provided with a narrow five bay north aisle in 1869. The rustic baluster font is of 1722. The old chest is unusually long. The stalls are partly 15th century and the timber framed lychgate is also medieval. On the north wall of the tower is a short reset length of Saxon frieze and two small 17th century figures from a monument. The porch was added in 1893.

Craswall Church

Font at Credenhill

CRASWALL *St Mary* SO 281363

This remote building has doorways of the 13th and 15th centuries and a 14th century east window. The belfry is partly old and there is seat outside the south and east walls. The west end was made into a lobby in the 18th century. Several windows are also of that period.

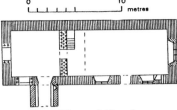

Plan of Craswall Church

CREDENHILL *St Mary* SO 450439

The nave has two 13th century north windows. The narrow chancel arch is early 13th century and is flanked by Victorian side-arches. The present chancel and the west tower are 14th century. The tall timber porch is 15th century. The nave roof is old and has an alternating pattern of tie-beams and collar-beams and a series of wind-braces. The font is dated 1667. There is some 14th century glass in a chancel window and one nave window contains old shields.

CROFT *St Michael* SO 451654

The church lies in front of the castle. It has a nave and chancel of c1300 with Y-tracery in the windows and a 17th century bell turret with miniture balusters and an ogee cap covered in lead. The late 17th century north doorway has an oval window over it. Against the chancel are remains of a chapel which once housed the monument of Sir Richard Croft, d1509, and his wife. There are box pews, an early 18th century west gallery, and medieval tiles, one dated 1456.

CUSOP *St Mary* SO 240415

Although much restored the nave is.Norman with a blocked original doorway with a huge lintel on the north side, one small south window, a plain chancel arch, and a font with saltire crosses and a trellis of lozenges. The chancel perhaps has Norman masonry too, but the lancets in the side walls are 13th century.

Croft Church

Dilwyn Church

DEWSALL   *St Michael*   SO 486335

Most of the features of the single chamber, including the timber porch and the font with ballflowers, are of the time of the consecration recorded in 1340.

DILWYN   *St Mary*   SO 415547

The original Norman nave lay where the south aisle and southern half of the nave now are. There is a big west tower of c1200 in line with where this nave would have been and the tower arch is partly blocked to provide an abutment for the five bay south arcade. Both the arcades and the rest of the present nave, aisles and chancel with clasping angle buttresses are 13th century. The north transept and the tomb recess with ballflowers in the chancel are of c1310-30 whilst the south porch is 16th century. The rood screen and parclose screens are medieval and in the south aisle are several coffin lids with foliated crosses and some 14th century tiles. Within the chancel is the effigy of a knight of c1320 and a 15th century indent with figures of a couple under canopies. It was filled with a type of cement or composition instead of brass.

DINEDOR   *St Andrew*   SO 534367

The short nave and chancel are of 1867-8 by Kempson but the west tower with a pyramidal roof has medieval masonry.

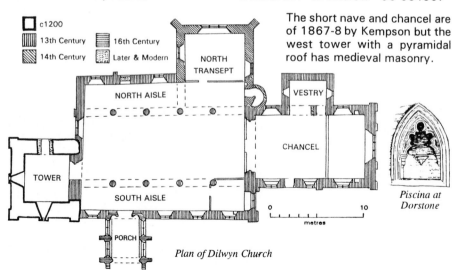

▢	c1200		
▦	13th Century	▤	16th Century
▧	14th Century	▨	Later & Modern

NORTH TRANSEPT

NORTH AISLE

VESTRY

TOWER

CHANCEL

SOUTH AISLE

PORCH

0 ⎣⎣⎣⎣⎣ 10
metres

Piscina at Dorstone

Plan of Dilwyn Church

DINMORE   *St John of Jerusalem*   SO 487504

A preceptory of the Knights of St John of Jerusalem was founded at Dinmore in 1189. The manor stands on the site of the preceptory buildings and the chapel doorway facing it is Norman. The rest of the chapel, which was originally longer, is 14th century. It has a west tower with a recessed spire. See page 103.

DOCKLOW   *St Bartholomew*   SO 564575

The west tower with a truncated pyramidal roof may be early 13th century. The single chamber may be late 13th century although the eastern part is rebuilt.

DONNINGTON   *St Mary*   SO 708343

A nave and chancel probably of c1300 were heavily restored and given a north aisle in 1862. There is a monument to E.H.Webb, d1655, with an inscription on drapery.

DORMINGTON   *St Peter*   SO 583402

The nave and chancel are probably 13th century. the chancel arch being of that date. Most of the windows were renewed in 1877 when the vestry and porch were added. More important is the Norman door knocker in the shape of a feline head. On the west wall is a feint wall painting of Christ in Majesty. There are tablets to Margaret Carpenter, d1666, and John Brydges, d1669.

DORSTONE   *St Faith*   SO 315418

The church was much restored in 1889. The chancel of c1300 has a double piscina with dogtooth ornament, two original windows, plus a 15th century window. The tower arch is 13th century.

DOWNTON-ON-THE-ROCK   *St Giles*   SO 428475

The old church ruin by the village has a narrow Norman chancel arch, two late 13th century chancel windows, and a 14th century window in the nave. The east and west end walls were rebuilt in the 19th century. A new church of 1861 designed by S.Pountney Smith lies in the grounds of Downton Castle.

DULAS   *St Michael*   SO 372294

Reassambled fragments of a Norman doorway from the old church form a garden gate north of Dulas Court. In the new church of 1865 are a pulpit, lectern, desk, and chairs which are all 17th century work.

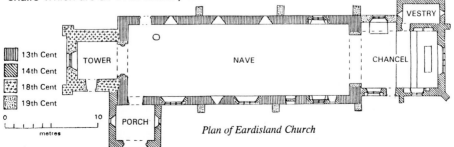

Plan of Eardisland Church

Eardisland Church   *Eardisley Church*

EARDISLAND   *St Mary*   SO 421585

The long nave has several early 13th century windows and doorways, the latter possibly repositioned. The porch and the two recesses for effigies are early 14th century. The chancel has sedilia and other features of c1300 and the vestry is contemporary. The tower was rebuilt in the 18th century. Under the Victorian tower arch is an old screen. In the nave is a 15th century incised slab with a foliated cross under an ogival canopy.

EARDISLEY   *St Mary Magdalene*   SO 313491

It would seem that the present nave constituted the whole of the Norman church. At the end of the 12th century a narrow south aisle and chapel were added with three arches towards the nave and just one towards what was then the chancel, now the nave east end. Between the two is a solid length of wall with a 14th century recess in it. In the 13th century a three bay north aisle was added. A new chancel beyond the original one was built c1300 and a north chapel with a two bay arcade towards the original chancel followed in the early 14th century. The arch connecting the east end of the chapel (now a vestry) with the chancel with Victorian. The south porch and south aisle windows are also 14th century. The tower at the west end of the north aisle was rebuilt in 1707.

In addition to its fascinating architectural history the church has a very fine and important Norman font of c1160. There are knot patterns on the stem whilst the bowl has a plaited band at the top and below a frieze of scenes, figures, and ornamentation mixed up with no divisions between them. The chief scenes show two knights in combat and the Harrowing of Hell with Christ frantically pulling a man out of a maze of tentacle-like twisted knots. There is also a splendid lion with long claws. In the nave are two helms of the 15th and 16th centuries respectively.

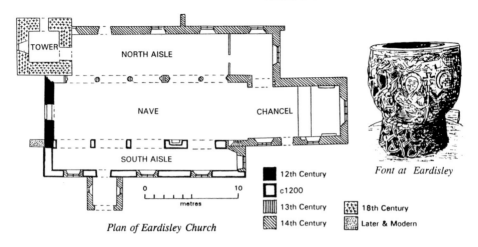

12th Century
c1200
13th Century
14th Century
18th Century
Later & Modern

0   10
metres

Plan of Eardisley Church

Font at Eardisley

EASTNOR   *St John*   SO 731372

The whole church was rebuilt by Sir George Gilbert Scott in 1852 except for the 14th century west tower, the Norman south doorway and eastern respond of the north arcade, plus the 13th century piers and arches of the arcade. There are many 18th and 19th century monuments, mostly to the Cocks family, Earls Somers.

EATON BISHOP   *St Michael*

SO 443391

The oblong west tower with two-light bell-openings is Norman. The broach spire is a later addition. The four bay arcades and narrow aisles are early 13th century, the NE window of the north aisle and the chancel are of c1300, and the SE window in the south aisle is slightly later. There are good reasons to believe that the very fine stained glass in several windows dates from c1330, its patron being Adam de Murimonth, Canon of Hereford and Cantor of Exeter from 1328. There is also a tablet to Richard Sneade, d1714.

Eaton Bishop Church

EDVIN LOACH   *St Mary*   SO 663585

East of the new church of c1860 by Sir George Gilbert Scott are ruins of the old church. It has an Early Norman south doorway and both south and north walls have extensive sections of herringbone masonry. The east end is 13th century and the thin west tower is 16th century.

EDVIN RALPH   *St Michael*   SO 645575

The nave and chancel form a single chamber with a trussed medieval roof. Both a Norman but the chancel, with one original window, may be slightly later. The nave has original doorways, that on the south being pointed with chequers on the capitals and having a stoup now fixed on the doorway jamb. Much of the south wall has been rebuilt. Two fine monuments with effigies of a late 13th century husband and wife, and an early 14th century husband and two wives of the Edefin family formerly lay in recesses in the chancel but now lie on the floor under the 13th century tower along with a tiny female effigy and an incised slab to Maud de Edefen, d1325. There are also 18th and 19th century tablets to the Burwall family.

ELTON   *St Mary*   SO 457710

The small Norman nave and chancel church by the hall has original doorways and one window. Other windows are 13th century and of the restoration of 1876. There is a Jacobean pulpit, a screen with 15th and 17th century parts, and Queen Elizabeth I's arms carved in wood.

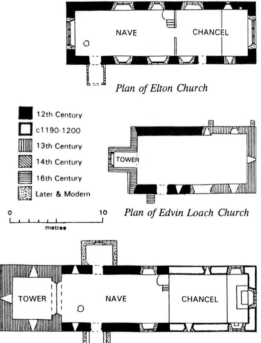

Plan of Elton Church

■	12th Century
□	c1190-1200
▥	13th Century
▨	14th Century
▤	16th Century
▦	Later & Modern

0 ⌐⌐⌐⌐⌐⌐⌐⌐⌐⌐ 10
metres

Plan of Edvin Loach Church

Effigies at Edvin Ralph

Plan of Edvin Ralph Church

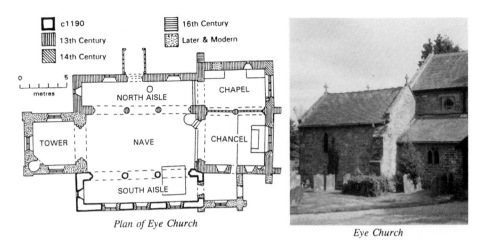

Plan of Eye Church

Eye Church

EVESBATCH *St Andrew*   SO 687482

The chancel and most of the nave windows are of 1877, but the nave is 14th century with a doorway and window of that date. The font cover is Jacobean and there are late medieval bench ends. Two females of the Dobyns family, d1658 and 1710, are commemorated by monuments, the former being a frontal demi-figure holding a baby.

EWYAS HAROLD *St Michael*   SO 387287

The 13th century west tower has a clasping stair turret at the SW corner and a south doorway. The tower arch dates from 1868 when the nave was rebuilt except for the thick walling below the north windows and the roof. The chancel of c1300 has an effigy of a lady holding her heart set in a tomb recess. The pulpit is Jacobean.

EYE *St Peter and St Paul*   SO 497638

The south aisle with a three bay arcade is of c1190, whilst the north aisle is of c1210-20, but both have later side windows. The early or mid 13th century chancel has a late 13th century north chapel and a 16th century east window. The nave clerestory of quatrefoil windows in niches and the tie-beam roof may be 14th century and the timber north porch is late 14th century. The west tower was mostly rebuilt in 1874. The pulpit looks Jacobean but is dated 1681 and there are benches with dolphin panels dated 1684. There are recumbent alabaster effigies on tomb chests of Sir Rowland Cornewall, d1520, and Sir Richard Cornewall, and his wife c1540.

EYTON *All Saints*   SO 475616

The single chamber has a Norman window and a 14th century window, others and the vestry being Victorian. There is a screen of c1500 with a panelled loft coving.

FAWLEY *St John*   SO 591295

The Norman nave and the chancel of 1827 are connected by a narrow arch flanked by Victorian openings. The nave south wall is a thin rebuild probably of the 14th century, when the present roof was built. There are fragments of an old screen. The scallops on the Norman font have probably been recut later.

Garway Church

FELTON   *St Michael*

SO 579485

Although mostly rebuilt in 1853 and given a spire in 1891, the church has old material in the nave, chancel, and west tower.

FORD   SO 512553

The small nave and apse of 1851 may be built on Norman foundations.

Fownhope Church

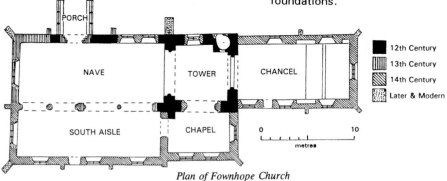

Legend:
- 12th Century
- 13th Century
- 14th Century
- Later & Modern

Plan of Fownhope Church

FOWNHOPE   *St Mary*   SO 582343

The Norman central tower has original belfry windows and arches to the east and west with chevrons. It has 13th and 14th century north windows. Also 14th century are the spire, the south aisle and chapel, the nave north windows (one has a Norman rere-arch) and the west part of the arcade. The other two bays of the arcade and the nave west wall are 13th century. The chancel with Y-tracery and intersecting tracery in the windows plus two tomb recesses, one with ballflowers, is of c1300-10. The fonts are of c1670 and the 18th century. A loose tympanum of c1150 shows a lion with the Virgin and Child, an incised slab with many inscriptions, and tablets to Johanna Lechmere, d1692, Nicholas Lechmere, d1711, and John Kidley c1720.

FOY   *St Mary*   SO 597284

The nave north doorway and chancel north window are 13th century. The west tower, the cusped recess of an altar beside the chancel arch, the south porch, and most of the windows are 14th century. Following the terms of John Abrahall's will of 1640 the east window is a copy then made of the medieval one at Sellack. His initials and the year 1673 appear on the gable, and the glass, also copied from Sellack, is dated 1675. The pulpit, screen, communion rail and stalls all incorporate 17th century work. The south door is 14th century. In the chancel and the nave altar recesses are two defaced late 13th century effigies with round objects at their feet. There are tablets to various members of the Abrahall family, George, d1673, Paul, d1675, and John, d1702.

GARWAY   *St Michael*   SO 455225

This church is unusually interesting. In the 1180s a preceptory of the Templars was founded here and excavations have laid bare part of the foundations of a round nave built in imitation of Holy Sepulchre church at Jerusalem. Also surviving are the chancel arch with two orders of colonettes and chevrons on trhe arch, and part of the north wall of what is assumed to have been an apsed chancel. The existing nave, the two bay arcade to a south chapel and the east end of the chancel are late 13th century. The chapel itself and the chancel east wall were rebuilt in the 16th century. A 17th century passageway-cum-porch connects the nave to an early 13th century NW tower with a pyramidal roof. This structure, set diagonally to the nave, and once detached, may have served as a strongpoint. Sculptured panels set on the outside of the nave are post-medieval. There are massive 16th or 17th century benches, stalls and panelling with Jacobean work, and a 17th century communion rail.

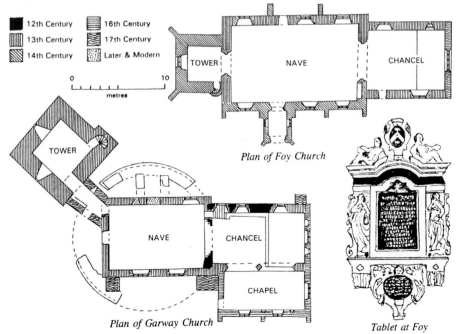

■ 12th Century	▤ 16th Century
▥ 13th Century	▧ 17th Century
▨ 14th Century	▦ Later & Modern

0 ⌊_⌊_⌊_⌊_⌊_⌋ 10
metres

TOWER   NAVE   CHANCEL

Plan of Foy Church

TOWER

NAVE   CHANCEL

CHAPEL

Plan of Garway Church

Tablet at Foy

Hampton Bishop Church

Goodrich Church

GOODRICH   *St Giles*   SO 573190

The church seems rather humble compared with the fine castle some distance away. The nave and chancel form a single chamber. The middle two bays of the six bay arcade are 13th century and the ends represent a lengthening c1300. The thin west tower with a lofty broach spire and the south porch are 14th century. The east window is 15th century. There is a a very damaged 13th century tomb chest.

GRAFTON   *St Peter*   SO 510371

A tablet to John Daubeney, d1741, from the ruined old church with a Norman doorway has been transferred to the new church of 1880 design by Kempson.

GRENDON BISHOP   *St John the Baptist*   SO 597564

This isolated church of 1787 in the fields was remodelled and given an apse in 1870. A Norman window is reset in the tower south wall.

HAMPTON BISHOP   *St Andrew*   SO 558380

The Norman nave has a south doorway with a large lintel with scale decoration and saltire crosses, a blank tympanum, an arch covered with chevrons, and a hoodmould with billets. Of 1190-1200 are the western extension of the nave, the north tower, and an arch between the chancel and north chapel. The last two parts are otherwise of c1300. East of the toweer is a 13th century aisle with a two bay arcade. In the chapel is a medieval reredos. The pulpit is partly Jacobean.

HATFIELD   *St Leonard*   SO 586594

The Early Norman nave north wall of herringbone masonry has a doorway with a tympanum decorated with a trellis pattern. The chancel is 13th century and the western part of the nave, now forming a lobby with a bell turret above, is 14th century. Part of the south wall is 17th century, and there are tablets of 1641, 1669, and 1673.

HENTLAND   *St Dubricius*

SO 543264

The nave and chancel and the north aisle with a four bay arcade all have features of c1300-50, whilst the west tower is later 14th century, but the whole was much restored by Seddon in 1853, and the vestry and north porch are Victorian. Of the 15th century are the font and three stained glass figures in the east window.

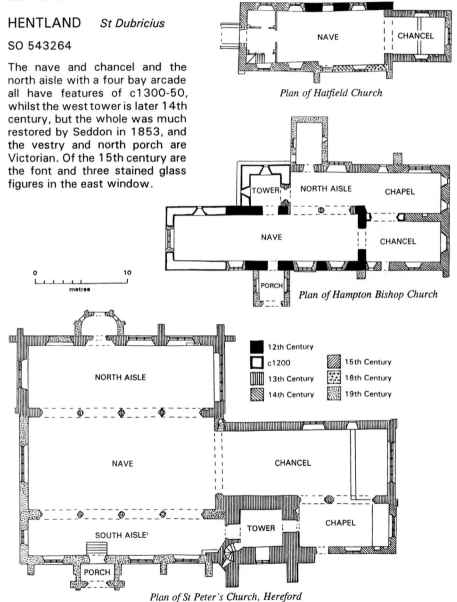

Plan of Hatfield Church

Plan of Hampton Bishop Church

	12th Century		
	c1200		15th Century
	13th Century		18th Century
	14th Century		19th Century

Plan of St Peter's Church, Hereford

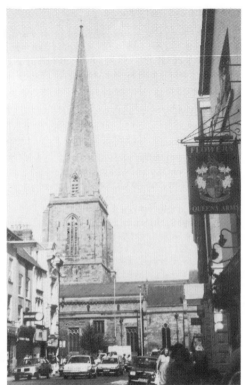

All Saints' Church, Hereford

St Peter's Church, Hereford

HEREFORD   *All Saints*   SO 508401

The oldest part of the church is the eastern respond of an early 13th century north aisle arcade exposed behind the respond of the present late 13th century arcade. By 1300 the aisle had been widened, given a large tower at the west end and a chapel to the east. The tower has a lofty spire. The south aisle and arcade are also late 13th century. Here the eastern respond was moved westwards in the 15th century when a stair turret to the rood loft was provided on this side. In the late 14th century the chancel was given a new east window. The wagon roof with bosses is slightly later. The south aisle has late 14th century windows and a shallow porch of that period has been transferred from the aisle to the south chapel. The north aisle has a hammerbeam roof for which the nave clerestory was abolished on the north side.

There are 14th century stalls with miserichords carved with various figures and creatures and a fine contemporary chest. The pulpit is an ornate piece dated 1621. In the south chapel is a reredos of c1700 with fluted Corinthian pilasters, and in the north aisle is a breadshelf of 1683. Of the 15th century are some tiles and a damaged mural painting of a large kneeling female figure. In the vestry formed from the eastern part of the south chapel is a 17th or 18th century hour-glass and a chained library.

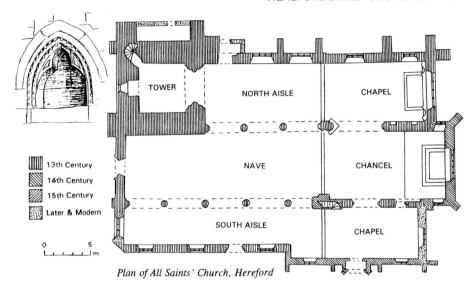

Plan of All Saints' Church, Hereford

13th Century
14th Century
15th Century
Later & Modern

0 ___ 5 m

TOWER

NORTH AISLE

CHAPEL

NAVE

CHANCEL

SOUTH AISLE

CHAPEL

HEREFORD   *St Peter*   SO 512400

The tower at the east end of the south aisle is late 13th century. The four bay arcades with slender quatrefoil piers, the chancel, chancel arch, and south chapel were all built c1300. The south aisle and arcade, the west front, and much else were rebuilt by Thomas Nicholson in 1880-5. There are several old roofs, that over the south chapel being low pitched with king-posts and traceried tie-beams. The 15th century stalls came from St Guthlac's priory. The miserichords are carved with roses. The organ case has panels of c1700, and there are carved royal arms of William III.

Hereford originally had three other medieval parish churches but those of St Martin and St Olave were destroyed during the siege of 1645 and St Nicholas was entirely rebuilt in 1842 to a design by Thomas Duckham.

Holme Lacy Church

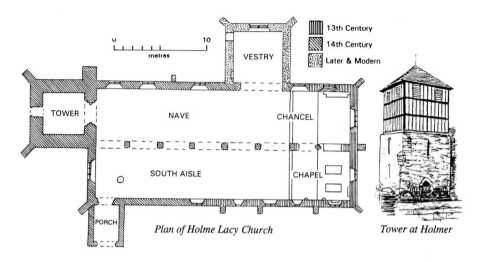

Plan of Holme Lacy Church   Tower at Holmer

HOLME LACY   *St Cuthbert*   SO 569347

The church has a long single main body and an equally long south aisle, both being covered with plaster tunnel vaults of the 1660s. The east end of the aisle was built first in the late 13th century with a two bay arcade and Y-traceried windows. The remaining six bays of the arcade, most of the windows, the south porch and the lower part of the west tower are all 14th century. The tower was completed in the 15th century and the vestry added in the 19th century.

The late 17th century font has acanthus and cherub's heads. There are 15th century stalls with various creatures carved on the miserichords, benches with Jacobean and late 17th century work, and fragments of old glass in a north window. In the south chapel are fine alabaster effigies of John Scudamore, d1571, and wife, and a marble monument with a sarcophagus and putti to Viscount Sligo, d1716. In the chancel is an early 18th century reclining effigy of James Scudamore, d1668, and a monument to Jame Scudamore, d1699.

HOLMER   *St Bartholomew*   SO 505424

The church comprises a large single chamber of c1190-1220 with a number of lancet windows, most of them renewed. Above the 19th century vestry at the west end is a 15th century window. The lower part of the detached south tower is early 13th century, the timber framed upper part being 16th century. The church has fine old roofs with scissor-braced single frames over the nave and hammerbeams and collar-beams of c1500 with tracery above both in the chancel. See plan on page 9.

HOPE MANSELL   *St Michael*   SO 626197

The nave north wall is Norman with 18th century windows. The east window and chancel arch are of c1300. Somewhat earlier are the chancel with lancets and the walling of a former aisle whose arcade has been removed so as to widen the nave. The south doorway is 14th century and the south porch is 17th century.

HOPE-UNDER-DINMORE   *St Mary*   SO 511528

The church was rebuilt by Kempson in 1879 and 1896 but it contains a 13th century font with Christ and various saints set under cinquefoiled arches, and an incised slab to Humfry Conyngsby, d1559, and his wife. There is a monument of c1760 to Earl Conyngsby and his wife and an infant son who choked to death on a cherry in 1708.

HOW CAPLE   *St Andrew and St Mary*   SO 612305

The chancel is 14th century and has a later low-pitched roof with bosses. The ashlar-faced west tower, nave, and south transept are all of 1693-5. One 14th century window is reset in the nave and the other windows are Victorian. The Late Norman font has vegetable and geometrical motifs. The pulpit is Jacobean and has a tester. There are two wings of an early 16th century German altarpiece with painting on both sides, carved Royal Arms of William III, and a screen with twisted columns and twisted arches also of the 1690s. There are numerous monuments to members of the Gregory family.

HUMBER   *St Mary*   SO 536564

The chancel with small lancets is of c1200 with a 14th century roof with tie-beams, king-posts, and cusped two way struts. The nave and the west tower with a broach spire are late 13th century, and the timber south porch is 14th century. The north chapel and several windows are of 1876-8. The Norman font has a rope moulding.

HUNTINGTON   *St Thomas Beckett*   SO 250534

The thickly walled single chamber is of c1300-20 but also has three renewed 16th century windows. The timber bell turret and the massive benches with roughly trefoiled ends are also 16th century.

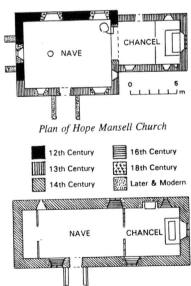

Plan of Hope Mansell Church

12th Century	16th Century
13th Century	18th Century
14th Century	Later & Modern

Plan of Huntington Church

How Caple Church

Plan of Kilpeck Church

Doorway carvings, Kilpeck

KENCHESTER   *St Michael*   SO 434433

The single chamber has two Norman windows at the east end of the side walls, doorways of c1200, an east window of c1300, and several small Victorian windows. A thickening of the west wall carries a 13th century double belfry. The chancel roof is Jacobean. The font may be an Early Norman remodelling of a Roman stone.

KENDERCHURCH   *St Mary*   SO 403284

The nave and chancel have medieval masonry but the features are of 1871 except the 16th century south doorway, a Norman font with chevrons, the chancel wagon-roof with small bosses, the Jacobean pulpit, and the top of the 15th century screen.

KENTCHURCH   *St Mary*   SO 419257

The church was entirely rebuilt in 1859 but contains semi-reclining effigies of John Scudamore, d1616, and his wife, plus their ten children.

KILPECK   *St Mary and St David*   SO 445305

The NE corner of the nave with long and short work is Saxon. The chancel has windows and a doorway of c1300 and the bellcote is of 1864. Otherwise this is a splendid and little altered Norman church of c1140-50 comprising a nave, square chancel, and an apse. It lies adjacent to the castle earthworks but may owe its unusually fine sculptured details to the presence here from 1134 of a small cell of the Benedictine abbey of Gloucester. All around the exterior are pilaster buttresses, some of which clasp the corners, and there is a corbel table. The many motifs carved on the corbels include The Lamb and Cross, two wrestlers, a sheila-na-gig and a dog and rabbit (all these are upon the apse). The south doorway has one order of colonettes carved with figures, thin trails and beast's heads, a tympanum with a Tree of Life, and arches with beakheads and linked medallions with dragons and birds. The chancel arch also has figures set one above the other on the colonettes, and chevrons. Further chevrons appear on the ribs of the vault over the apse and on the arches of the nook-shafted apse windows. The stoup with four animal heads and two hands gripping two heads, and the large plain font are also 12th century work.

KIMBOLTON   *St James*   SO 526616

The chancel is Norman and has two original small windows. Some of the nave masonry may also be Norman (see the one small north window) but otherwise the nave, west tower, and south transept are all 13th century. Several windows and the transept and tower arches were renewed in the 19th century, when the porch was added. The tower has belfry openings with plate tracery and is covered with a tall shingled broach spire. The stall backs with linenfold panels are early 16th century. The oldest of the tablets in the south transept is one of 1766 to the Wanklin family.

Kilpeck Church

Interior, Kilpeck Church

KING'S CAPLE   *St John the Baptist*   SO 559289

The earliest feature is the late 13th century window and recess on the south side of the large nave. The lower parts of the tower and several windows in the nave and chancel are 14th century. Of the 15th century are the upper part of the tower with a recessed spire, several other windows, and the south porch and the Aramstone chapel on the north side, both with octapartite rib-vaults.

Kingsland Church

Kingsland Church

KINGSLAND   *St Michael*   SO 447614

The west tower, the long aisled nave with five bay arcades, the chancel and north vestry, and the north porch with a tiny chapel east of it with a tomb recess between it and the aisle, are all of c1300-50. The porch entrance is like half of an octogan and cusped. The nave roof has tie-beams, king-posts, and four-way struts. The chancel has a low painted ceiling. The only later portions are the 15th century tower top and the timber south porch, plus the 16th century upper storey of the vestry.

King's Pyon Church

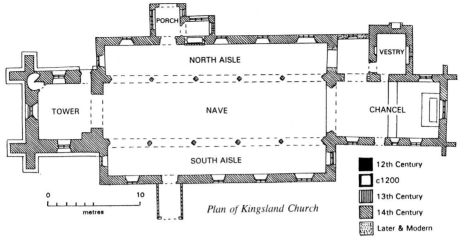

Plan of Kingsland Church

■ 12th Century
□ c1200
▒ 13th Century
▨ 14th Century
▦ Later & Modern

KING'S PYON   *St Mary*   SO 438507

Part of the nave north wall is Early Norman. The south doorway with trumpet capitals on the shafts and the keeled chancel arch responds are of c1180-1200, when the church was rebuilt and lengthened. The priest's doorway and south transept are late 13th century. The tomb recess in the transept is early 14th century and contains late 14th century effigies of a knight and lady. The west tower and vestry are also 14th century. The north transept and the organ space are of 1872. Each has an older window reset in it. See plan on page 9.

KINGSTONE   *St Michael*   SO 424357

The eastern part of the nave and the south doorway are Norman. A north aisle with a three bay arcade was added c1200-10, and in 1200-40 the chancel was rebuilt and a two bay north chapel was added to it. In c1300 the aisle was widened and a tower built west of it, and then c1330 the nave was given an ashlar-faced extension ending flush with the tower west wall. There are lancets in the chapel and a late 13th century window in the nave but the other windows are mostly of c1330-40. The church has a plain Norman font and a chest dug out of a single tree trunk.

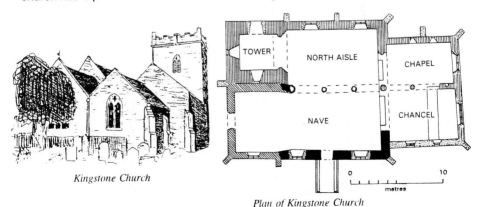

Kingstone Church

Plan of Kingstone Church

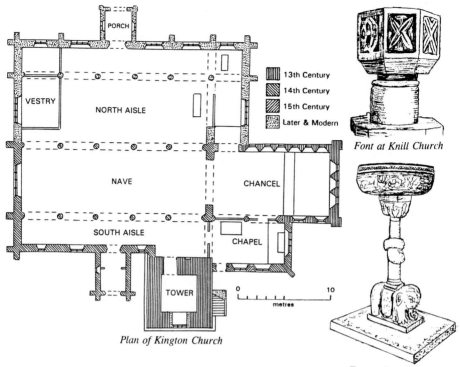

Font at Knill Church

Plan of Kington Church

Font at Lea Church

KINGTON   *St Mary*   SO 292567

The church lies on a hill west of the town. The oldest part is the keep-like tower of c1200 in a transeptal position on the south side which was originally detatched. The early 13th century chancel is a fine structure with three lancets in the east wall and six in the north wall. The window with Y-tracery on the south side must be of c1290-1300. In c1300-20 the nave was rebuilt and provided with narrow aisles with five bay arcades, and in the 1330s a chapel was built on the south side of the chancel. The two bay arcade of the chapel and one window are 15th century insertions. In 1874 the church was enlarged by greatly widening the north aisle and adding a narrow outer north aisle with its own north porch. The font is Norman and has a rope moulding and chevrons. In the chapel are alabaster effigies on a tomb chest of Thomas Vaughan, d1469, and his wife, and there is also a substantial tablet to William Mathews, d1688, in the south aisle.

KINNERSLEY   *St James*   SO 346497

The striking feature of the church is the saddleback-roofed 14th century tower projecting west beyond the north aisle. The nave west wall and doorway are Norman. The chancel is of c1300, the aisles and timber south porch are of c1300-30. In the 15th century the four bay south arcade was renewed and a rood stair turret built at the east end of it. The north vestry is Victorian. The reredos and stalls have Jacobean panels and the pulpit has Flemish allegorical figures of c1530. In the chancel is a brass to the priest William Leviot, d1421. Above are kneeling figures of Francis Smallman, d1635 and wife, with a baldacchino upon cherubs with trumpets. See p9.

KINSHAM   *All Saints*   SO 364649

The renewed windows suggest a date of c1280-1300 for the single chamber, but one window on the south may be older. There are fragments of old glass in the east window, some elementary 18th century woodwork, and a tablet to Thomas Harley, d1738.

KNILL   *St Michael*   SO 291604

The nave and chancel masonry is Norman, with one original north window in the chancel. The short west tower and the south doorway are 13th century, and the octagonal font with knots, crosses, etc, in framed panels maybe of c1200. Other features are Victorian.

Kinnersley Church

LAYSTERS   *St Andrew*   SO 568633

The nave has a Norman south doorway with a roll-moulded shouldered lintel and tympanum and a blocked original north window. The chancel is 13th or 14th century, the west tower is early 13th century, and the nave roof with arched braces going up to collar-beams is 14th century. All the windows are Victorian.

LEA   *St John the Baptist*   SO 658217

The wide north aisle and the chancel were rebuilt by the Victorians. The aisle west window, one south window, and the spire and tower top are 14th century. The tower base is late 13th century, and the three bay north arcade, the north chapel, and the east window are of the time of the rebuilding of 1418. There are portions of an old screen, and a large chest dug-out from a trunk. More notable is the font which is an Italian stoup of c1180-1200 given to the church in 1907. The bowl has a frieze of foliage with human figures and animals and stands on a shaft borne by an elephant.

Kington Church

LEDBURY   *St Michael*   SO 713377

This is the largest purely parochial church in Herefordshire. From a large Norman church as long as the present building there remain the pier bases of a north arcade and the chancel with two complete windows and parts of others, clasping corner buttresses, and two bay arcades for side chapels. The nave arcades were renewed c1200 and a new west doorway then provided with chevrons and keeled arches. The large detached tower to the north is early 13th century but the recessed spire and upper parts were rebuilt in 1727 by Nathaniel Wilkinson.

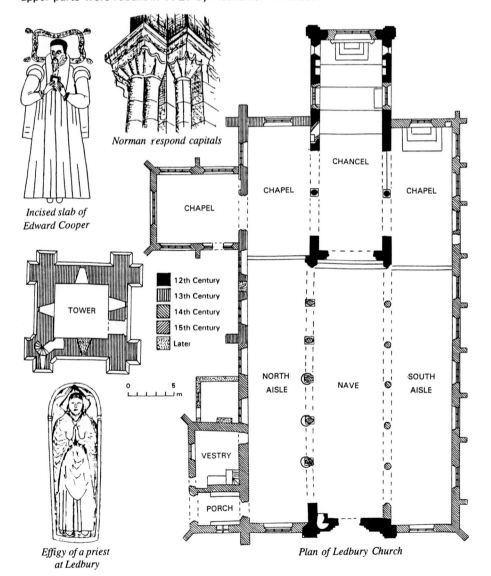

Norman respond capitals

Incised slab of Edward Cooper

TOWER

■ 12th Century

▥ 13th Century

▨ 14th Century

▨ 15th Century

▦ Later

0   5
└─┴─┴─┴─┴─┘ m

Effigy of a priest at Ledbury

CHANCEL

CHAPEL   CHAPEL   CHAPEL

CHAPEL

NORTH AISLE   NAVE   SOUTH AISLE

VESTRY

PORCH

Plan of Ledbury Church

Interior of Ledbury Church

Most of the exterior dates from c1280-1340 when the aisles were widened, the north aisle being treated first. The aisles have roofs of this period with arched braces to collar-beams and curved wind-braces. Beyond the north chapel is a large outer chapel with huge four-light windows studded with ballflowers. The arcade piers were again renewed, but the arches still remain from c1200-10. The two storey NW porch and the adjacent vestry are late 14th century.

The stalls are 16th century. Fragments of 13th and 15th century glass appear in several windows. In the chancel are demi-figures of Thomas Thornton, Master of St Katherine's Hospital, d1629, and John Hoskins, rector, d1631, plus kneeling figures of Edward Skinner, d1631, and his wife. There are brasses to William Calwe, a kneeling early 15th century priest, Thomas Capel, d1490, and John Hayward, d1614, plus an incised slab to Edward Cooper, d1596. In the south chapel is a bust and a trophy to Captain Samuel Skynner, d1725. In the north chapel is a fine but damaged female effigy of c1360. A late 13th century effigy of a priest lies in the outer north chapel.

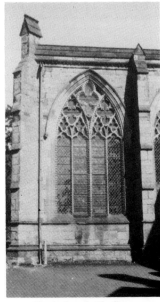

North chapel at Ledbury

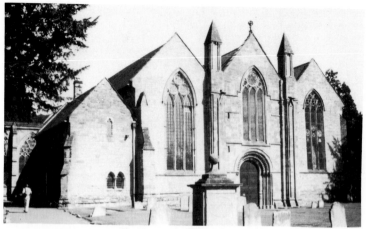

West front of Ledbury Church

LEINTHALL EARLS   *St Andrew*   SO 443679

The single chamber has a Norman west doorway and windows near the east end, an east window of c1800, other later windows, a timber framed west gable, and an old tie-beam roof with queen-posts.

LEINTHALL STARKES   *St Mary Magdalene*   SO 442700

The doorways and three windows of the single chamber are Norman. On the south side are late 13th and 15th century windows. The double bellcote is 17th century, and there is an old roof. A buttress now blocks a former west doorway.

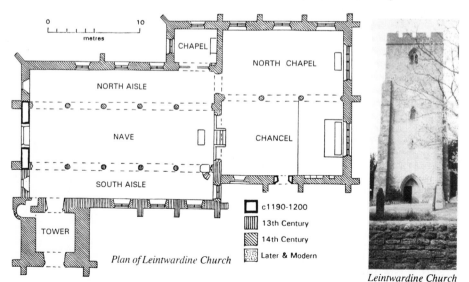

Plan of Leintwardine Church

Leintwardine Church

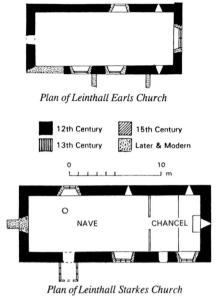

Plan of Leinthall Earls Church

| ■ | 12th Century | ▨ | 15th Century |
| |||| 13th Century | ▦ | Later & Modern |

0   10
L_I_I_I_I_I_____I m

NAVE   CHANCEL

Plan of Leinthall Starkes Church

Leintwardine Church

LEINTWARDINE   *St Mary Magdalene*   SO 404741

The nave west wall and doorway and the reset priest's doorway are of c1190-1200. The five bay south arcade and aisle are late 13th century. Of the 14th century are the north aisle, the wide chancel, the north chapel, the transeptal chapel west of the last, and the lofty SW tower with a porch below it. The north windows were provided with new tracery in the 15th century when the nave was given a clerestory and a low pitched roof with many bosses. The chancel arch and south windows were renewed in the 19th century. On either side of the main east window are remains of a late medieval reredos and there are stalls probably brought here from Wigmore Abbey.

Interior of Leominster Priory Church

LEOMINSTER   *St Peter and St Paul*   SO 498598

A nunnery existing at Leominster in the 9th century was dissolved in 1046. A Benedictine priory dependant on Reading Abbey was founded here in 1123. The eastern parts of the church must have been complete by 1130 when a nave altar was consecrated. Composed of transepts with east apses and a chancel with an ambulatory with radiating chapels, these parts were destroyed after the priory was dissolved in the 1530s. Little remains of the monastic buildings north of the church, but the nave survives with important work of c1130-50. It seems the arcades were originally designed with arches alternating with solid sections of walling, a layout suggesting domes may have been intended. Before long this scheme was abandoned and part of the layout was replaced by three adjacent arches on each side with round piers. There is a fine Norman west doorway and a west tower may have then existed, although the present tower is 15th century. The nave still stands because its south aisle was used by the parish. The aisle was widened in the 13th century, given a huge new west window in the 15th century,, and was doubled in size by the addition c1310 of a wide aisle with large four-light windows adorned with ballflowers. The arcade between the two spaces is of 1872 replacing Tuscan pillars inserted after a fire of 1699 which destroyed the medieval furnishings. There are some 14th century tiles in the parochial nave, a wall-painting of a Wheel of Life of c1275 on the north wall of the monastic nave, and an old ducking stool in the north aisle.

Now part of the town, but originally lying NE of the priory precinct gateway is the Forbury Chapel, which probably dates from the 1280s and was dedicated to St Thomas of Canterbury. The east window, the cusped lancets in the side walls, and the south doorway are all original. After the Reformation the chapel was used as a courthouse, then a school, and then in modern times became an office.

Interior of Leominster Priory Church

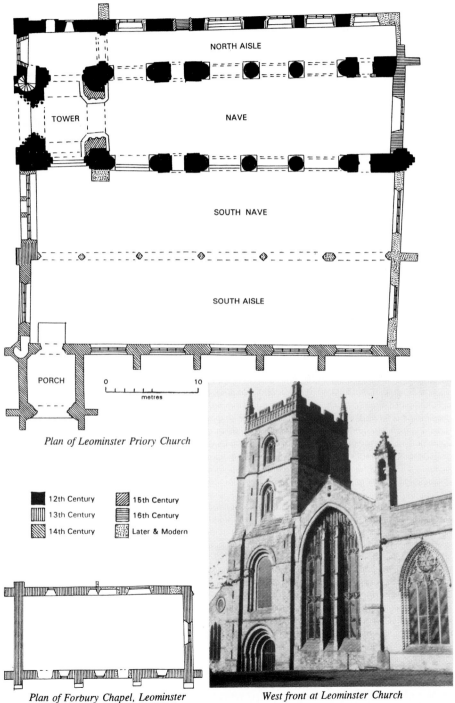

Plan of Leominster Priory Church

12th Century
13th Century
14th Century
15th Century
16th Century
Later & Modern

Plan of Forbury Chapel, Leominster

West front at Leominster Church

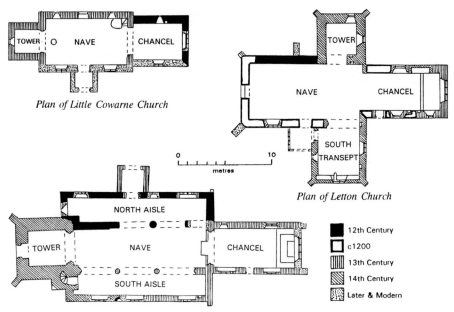

Plan of Little Cowarne Church

Plan of Letton Church

Plan of Linton-by-Ross Church

■	12th Century
□	c1200
▥	13th Century
▨	14th Century
▦	Later & Modern

LETTON   *St John the Baptist*   SO 335464

The nave has Early Norman herringbone masonry on the north side. Of c1180-1200 is the rest of the nave with a south doorway with a lintel with rosettes and chevrons on the jambs, and a west doorway with a tufa frieze and tympanum. The chancel is of c1300, and the north tower and the south transept with a tomb recess with ballflowers are 14th century. The south door with fine metalwork is Late Norman, the plain chancel benches are 17th century. The pulpit and test and the reader's desk are 18th century work from Bristol.

LINGEN   *St Michael*   SO 366672

The stone parts of the tower and the benches are 16th century. The rest is of 1891. Inside is a small tablet to John Downes, d1687.

LINTON-BY-ROSS   *St Mary*   SO 660254

The masonry and two bay arcade of the north aisle, and one reset jamb of a south doorway are Norman. The chancel, the south aisle and the north doorway are 13th century. The porch is 14th century. The north wall remains of a Norman west tower which was replaced by a west entension of the nave in the 14th century when the south aisle was also extended westwards and a new west tower added on. The chancel east wall is 19th century. There are tablets to John Elmehurst, d1662, and the Reverend Peter Senhouse, d1760, plus a fine 13th century floriated cross-slab.

LITTLE BIRCH   *St Mary*   SO 505325

A Norman font lies within the church, which was rebuilt in 1869 by W.Chick.

Little Hereford Church

Letton Church

LITTLE COWARNE   *Dedication Unknown*   SO 602512

The church was mostly rebuilt in 1869 by Kempson, and the porch is of 1911. Parts of the chancel, with one window, are Norman. Of the 13th century are the west tower with a saddleback roof, and the nave north wall, with one original lancet.

LITTLE DEWCHURCH   *St David*   SO 529318

Except for the 14th century west tower with a pointed tunnel vault over the bell chamber, the church was entirely rebuilt in 1869 by Preedy.

LITTLE HEREFORD   *St Mary Magdalene*   SO 554680

A small section of the nave north wall with one small window is Norman. Otherwise the nave and the pyramidal roofed west tower are all 13th century. Of the 14th century are two nave windows, the two tomb recesses in the south wall, the narrow chancel arch with the rood stair leading off it, and most of the chancel including two more recesses, one of which contains a contemporary female effigy.

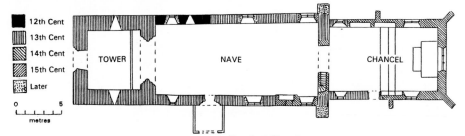

Plan of Little Hereford Church

LLANCILLO   *St Peter*   SO 366256

The small church lies beside Llancillo Court. The chancel has a Norman window and tufa quoins. The east window is 13th century. Two other windows and the porch are probably 17th century. The chancel arch and two windows are Victorian. The font is dated 1632 and has arabesque panels, and there is a 13th century dug-out chest.

LLANDINABO   *St Dinabo*   SO 518284

The church was entirely rebuilt in 1881 by A.Lloyd Oswell, leaving a fine screen of c1520 with a band of dolphins on the cornice, the partly Jacobean pulpit, and the brass to Thomas Tompkins, a child who accidentally drowned in 1629 and is thus depicted standing in a pool.

LLANGARRON   *St Deinst*   SO 530211

The west tower with a recessed spire, the chancel with a scissor-braced roof, and the nave south doorway are 14th century. The font, the priest's doorway and a south window are 15th century. Other windows are later, and the north arcade and wide north aisle are 19th century. The stone with interlace reset on the SE buttress is Norman. The pulpit is Jacobean. There is 17th century work in the communion rail. There are tablets to Johan Philpott de Sonke, d1689, Rowland Scudamore, d1697, William Gwllym, d1698, and Mrs Audley, d1715, and a small 13th century effigy.

LLANROTHAL   *St John the Baptist*   SO 471185

The nave now lies derelict and empty. It has a Norman north wall and a south wall of c1300 with remains of a porch. The late 13th century chancel has been restored for further use. It has a 15th century south window and a Victorian vestry.

LLANVEYNOE   *St Peter*   SO 304314

The single chamber is medieval but has 19th and 20th century windows. There are two 11th century panels, one with a crude depiction of the Crucifixion.

Llanwarne Church

Brass to Thomas Tompkins at Llandinabo Church

LLANWARNE *St John the Baptist* SO 506282

This church now lies in ruins, having been replaced by a new church of 1864 (Christ Church) to the west, in which now lies the 17th century font. The nave north wall and the arch to the rebuilt north chapel are 13th century. The south aisle with a four bay arcade is 14th century. The west tower is 15th century, the chancel east bay is 16th century, and the south doorway and porch are 17th century. See page 14.

LONGTOWN *St Peter* SO 321291

This church was mostly rebuilt in 1868. It is converted into a house. Both the nave and the chancel with one lancet are probably 13th century. The east window is 14th century and the single framed collar-beam roof over the chancel is dated 1640.

LUCTON *St Peter*

SO 437642

A tablet to John Pierrepont, d1711, lies in the church of 1850.

LUGWARDINE

St Peter SO 552410

The 13th century chancel has a row of four lancets in the north wall. The thick walling of the eastern part of the north aisle is a relic of the base

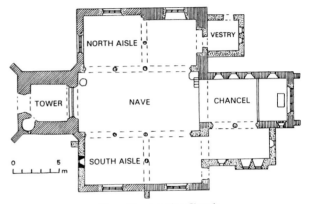

Plan of Lugwardine Church

of 13th century north tower. Otherwise the aisle outer walls and the west tower are 15th century, but the south aisle west wall has a Norman west window reset in what is probably a 17th or 18th century rebuilding. Most of the windows of the church, the vestries and the arcades are of Kempson's restoration of 1871-2. There is a brass to Jane Best, d1622, a semi-reclining effigy of William Reed, d1634, and a semi-reclining figure of the rector John Best, Jane's husband, d1637.

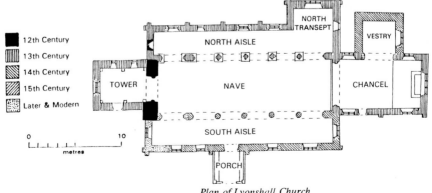

12th Century
13th Century
14th Century
15th Century
Later & Modern

Plan of Lyonshall Church

Lyonshall Church

Madley Church

LYONSHALL   *St Michael*   SO 331562

The north arcade has five bays of c1250 and a slightly later west bay constructed after a Norman west tower had been replaced by a new rectangular tower beyond it. The west wall of the original tower still survives, with one Norman window. The south wall also survived until 1872 when Bodley added a west bay to the south arcade of c1300. The chancel and north transept and one south aisle window are also of c1300. The other windows, vestry, and timber porch are Victorian. The font is partly 13th century and there is a headless 13th century effigy of a civilian.

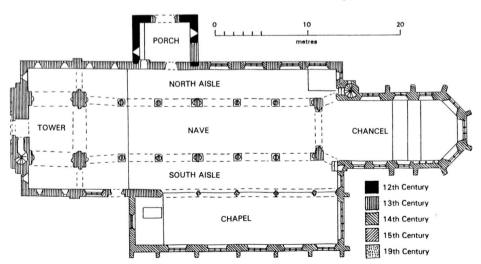

Plan of Madley Church

MADLEY   *Nativity of the Virgin*   SO 420388

Madely has a large, attractive, and interesting church. The north porch is obviously Norman except for the inner and outer doorways and was originally the north transept of a cruciform and aisless church. Early in the 13th century a west tower was begun, aisles added with western bays engaging the tower, and the church greatly lengthened to the east. The arcades have three bays between the tower and the position of the Norman chancel arch, where there are wider piers, and then another three bays beyond that. Small 13th century windows remain in the outer walls of the western part with a doorway on the south side with a 15th century window beside it. By 1318 a wide new chancel which further lengthened the church was under construction. It has polygonal ends to both east and west and is built over a vaulted crypt reached by steps on the south side. In c1330 the wide outer south aisle or Chilston Chapel was begun. This has an arcade of five bays and uses the west wall of the former Norman transept for its west end. There are abaci with ballflowers on the piers and windows with reticulated tracery which have counterparts inserted in the north aisle east of the porch. Although now quite light inside, the church would have been dark when it still had all its medieval glass, of which now only a few fragments remain in the east window and in the aisle side windows.

The large font under the tower is probably Norman. The parclose screen in the north aisle is 17th century with older parts. There are stalls with miserichords in the chancel. The west door and the tower staircase door have 13th century ironwork. Above the chancel arch are traces of a wall-painting. On a tomb chest in the chapel are recumbent effigies of Richard Willison, d1575, and his wife, and in the chancel are kneeling figures of Peter Garnons, d1626, and his wife. In the chapel is a 17th or 18th century reredos.

Interior of Madley Church

MANSELL GAMAGE   *St Giles*   SO 394445

The south doorway is of c1200 and is covered by a late medieval timber porch with cusped and traceried bargeboards. Several windows and the south transept are of c1300. The north transept, the east window, and several other features are of 1877, whilst the west tower is of 1824. The church is now used as a private house.

MANSELL LACY   *St Michael*   SO 426456

The blocked north doorway shows that the nave is Norman. The south aisle with a three bay arcade and the chancel are 13th century. The west tower, the south porch, and the whole east wall are 14th century. One of the original chancel windows is reset in the 19th century vestry. In the chancel are tablets of 1676 and 1691.

MARDEN   *St Mary*   SO 512471

The four bay arcades and the font date from c1280-1300. The aisle outer walls were rebuilt in 1856 but the south doorway is partly original. More memorable are the 14th century parts, a tower set to the north of the west end of the north aisle and an apsed chancel. The tower has a recessed spire and its own external doorway.

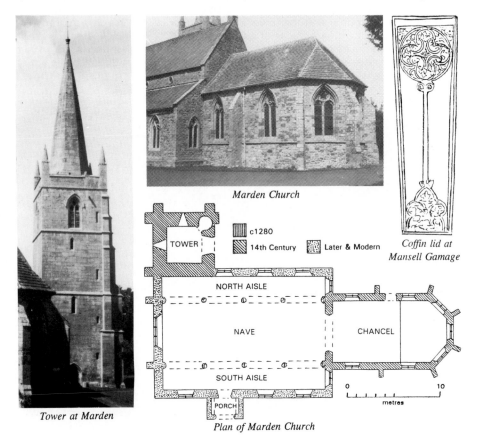

Marden Church

Coffin lid at Mansell Gamage

c1280
14th Century   Later & Modern

TOWER

NORTH AISLE

NAVE   CHANCEL

SOUTH AISLE

PORCH

0   10
metres

Tower at Marden

Plan of Marden Church

MATHON   *St John the Baptist*   SO 734458

Sections of herringbone masonry and two doorways with plain tympani only decorated with rope mouldings remain of the small Early Norman nave and apse. In the late 12th century the building was extended at both ends to form a long single chamber and the east windows and priest's doorway are of that period. A north window is 13th century and a south window is of c1300, whilst the others are Victorian. The west tower, the timber south porch, and the nave roof with tie-beams and collar-beams are all probably late 14th century.. There are two effigies on a tomb chest of John Walweyn, d1617, and her husband.

MICHAELCHURCH   *St Michael*   SO 522256

The church is said to have been founded in 1056 by Bishop Herwald of Llandaff but the earliest features of the single chamber are the pair of east windows and north doorway of c1200. Several other windows are of the same period or slightly later, the south doorway may be of c1300, and there is one 15th century south window. The Norman font has a knot frieze, saltire crosses, and interlaced arches. The frame of the screen is old, and there is 13th century feigned ashlaring painted on the walls. In the north wall is an inscribed Roman altar partly cut back to form a rough capital.

MICHAELCHURCH ESCLEY   *St Michael*

SO 307342

The Norman nave and the 16th century chancel form a single chamber. One window is 15th century, three windows are 17th century, and the south doorway is 18th century although the porch in front of it is 16th century. The wagon roof with small bosses is late medíeval. The west tower and three of the chancel windows are Victorian. On the north wall is a mural painting of Christ and the tools of the trades.

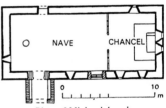

Plan of Michaelchurch

MIDDLETON-ON-THE-HILL   *St Mary*

SO 541646

The 13th century west tower is large compared with the Norman nave and chancel with pilaster buttresses, several original windows and doorways with chevrons on the arches. Three windows are late 13th century and the east window of c1300 is from Pudleston church. The font with a chevron band is also Norman.

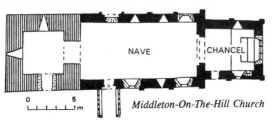

Middleton-On-The-Hill Church

Mathon Church

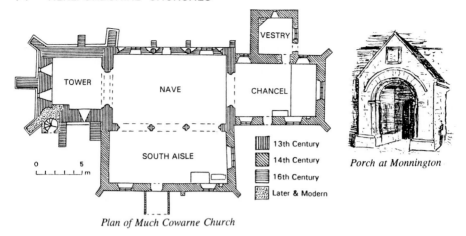

Porch at Monnington

Plan of Much Cowarne Church

13th Century
14th Century
16th Century
Later & Modern

MOCCAS *St Michael* SO 357434

This is an all-Norman church of tufa comprising a nave, square chancel, and an apse still with its original windows. The nave doorways of sandstone have one order of shafts, and tympani, now very worn. That on the south was a Tree of Life, whilst on the north was a beast and scrolls. Of the 14th century are the timber porch, four windows with remains of contemporary glass, the effigy of a cross-legged knight, and perhaps also the bellcote. See plan on page 9.

MONKLAND *All Saints* SO 460577

The nave has two Norman windows on each side but has been refaced. Two north windows and the west tower are late 13th century. Two south windows and the doorway are 14th century. Street rebuilt the chancel in 1866.

MONNINGTON-ON-WYE *St Mary* SO 374434

The 15th century west tower has large battlements with cruciform arrow-slits. The rest of the church, comprising nave, chancel, and a north porch, was rebuilt for Uvedale Tomkyns in 1679. The screen, communion rail, pulpit, font, panelling, benches, and the finely carved arms of Charles II are all of that date. There is a ledger stone to Uvedale Tomkyns and bust of Robert Perrot, d1667. See page 76.

MORDIFORD *Holy Rood* SO 571375

The nave has a Norman south doorway with one order of shafts and chevrons on the arch, and reset in the vestry is a doorway of c1200. A central tower and a new chancel were added in the 13th century. A new tower projecting from the west end of the nave south wall was built c1811 and the upper parts of the original tower then removed. The north aisle, the small chapel opening off the nave, and most of the windows are of the late 19th century.

MORETON JEFFRIES *Dedication Unknown* SO 604485

The single chamber has a 14th century doorway, a chancel roof with beams and raking struts, and a 17th century pulpit and tester.

Moccas Church

Much Dewchurch Church

MORETON-ON-LUGG   *St Andrew*   SO 505456

Rebuilding in 1867 by W.H.Knight left only a Norman window in the chancel, the late medieval three bay arcade and aisle eastern window, the single framed collar-beam nave roof, and the screen with a band of running vine on the cornice and cresting.

MUCH BIRCH   *St Mary and St Thomas*   SO 504305

The church was rebuilt by Thomas Foster in 1837 but has a mid 17th century chest in the vestry and the lower part of a 14th century churchyard cross shaft.

MUCH COWARNE   *St Mary*   SO 618472

A late Norman doorway is reset in the central arch of the blocked three bay arcade of a 13th century north aisle demolished in the 16th century. The west tower is probably early 13th century but one window looks Norman, the buttresses and north wall are 16th century, and a new stair turret was provided after the spire was destroyed by lightning in 1840. The wide south aisle and three bay arcade, the chancel, and perhaps the vestry are of c1300. The east window is late 14th century. In the aisle is a late 13th century effigy of a knight and a tomb chest with recumbent effigies of Edmund Fox, d1617, and wife. On the sides are ten kneeling children and three babies in a cradle. An effigy of Sybil Reed, d1624, lies in the chancel.

MUCH DEWCHURCH   *St David*   SO 483311

The nave and chancel are both Norman. Three original windows still remain partially or wholly, plus the plain chancel arch and south doorway with a tympanum. The west tower is 13th century. There are several south windows of c1280-1320, and the east window is late 14th century. The pyramidal roof of the tower, the north aisle and its two bay arcade, and the vestry are all Victorian. The porch is 14th century. The Norman font has arcading, small heads and flowers, and the pulpit is Jacobean. Part of a foliated 13th century coffin lid forms a shaft by the altar. There are recumbent effigies of c1570 to John and Walter Pye, kneeling figures of Walter Pye, d1625, and his wife, and a tablet to John Symons, d1763.

Much Marcle Church

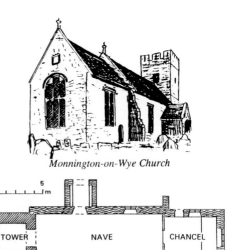

Monnington-on-Wye Church

Plan of Monnington-on-Wye Church

MUCH MARCLE   *St Bartholomew*   SO 657327

Although the south doorway and the aisle outer walls may be slightly later, the four bay arcades are both of c1230-40 and there is a clerestory of single lancets above. Several windows with Y-tracery are of c1300 and about that time the chancel was extended and provided with a chapel with a two bay arcade. The chancel was given a new classical style priest's doorway in the 18th century, and in the 19th century the chapel north wall was rebuilt and a vestry added alongside. There are indications of older arches on either side of the 15th century central tower so an older tower and transepts may once have existed. The communion rail is late 17th century and there is a heraldic panel of 1628 in the north chapel east window. The recess in the north wall of the chancel contains a fine effigy of Blanche Mortimer, Lady Grandison, d1347. In the south aisle is an oak effigy of a man of c1370. In the north chapel are a tomb chest with two effigies of c1400, and a black and white marble tomb chest with effigies of Sir John Kyrle, d1650, and his wife.

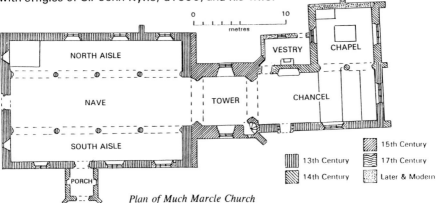

Plan of Much Marcle Church

MUNSLEY   *St Bartholomew*   SO 663410

The nave and chancel are both Early Norman with original windows, a plain chancel arch, and herringbone masonry in the east wall. The illegible inscription slab in the south wall may be Saxon or Early Norman. Other windows and the nave doorways are 14th century.

NEWTON   *St John the Baptist*

SO 347329

The church was rebuilt in 1842 but contains a pulpit of c1660.

12th Cent
14th Cent
Later

0   3
m

O   NAVE   CHANCEL

Plan of Munsley Church

NORTON CANON   *St Nicholas*   SO 382478

The NW tower with clasping buttresses and a pyramidal roof is 13th century. The nave, chancel, and shallow transwepts are of brick and were under construction in 1718. Reset in them are windows of c1300 from the medieval church. Two contain contemporary glass of the grisaille type. The communion rail, pulpit, and reredos all incorporate early 17th century material.

OCLE PYCHARD   *St James*   SO 596463

The eastern part of the nave and the south doorway are perhaps 13th century. The western third of the nave, the chancel, and the NE vestry are all 14th century. The west wall has a doorway flanked by buttresses both inside and outside which support a tiny tower. The copper covered broach spire on the tower is fairly recent.

ORCOP   *St Mary*   SO 474263

The west tower has a weatherboarded timber upper storey with heavy timbers supporting it inside. The narrow north aisle and its three bay arcade are early 13th century and there is a late 13th century window in the chancel. The south doorway is 14th century. Other windows and the polygonal vestry are of 1860 by Thomas Nicholson. The nave has a fine old wagon roof. In the chancel is part of a Norman scalloped pillar piscina.

ORLETON   *St George*   SO 495673

The nave is Norman and has an original west window, now blocked by the 13th century tower. The tower doorway of c1200 is probably reset. The early 13th century chancel has several lancet windows. The chancel arch and the tie-beam roof with king-posts and queen-posts may be 14th century. The vestry is Victorian. The Late Norman font has nine apostles standing under arches. There are two 13th century dug-out chests, some fragments of 14th century glass in the nave windows, and a fine mid-17th century pulpit. See page 16.

Orleton Church

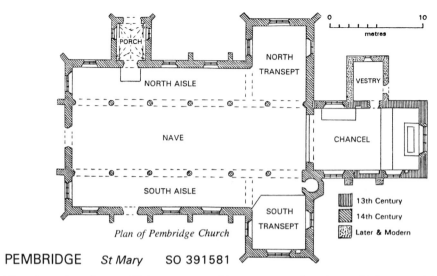

Plan of Pembridge Church

13th Century
14th Century
Later & Modern

PEMBRIDGE   St Mary   SO 391581

The chancel walls are 13th century and have traces of arches which opened into former chapels, but the windows and the whole of the rest of the church are of c1320-60. There are transepts and aisles with six bay arcades above which are circular and cinquefoiled clerestory windows, a vaulted north porch, and a rood stair turret covered with a pinnacle beside the chancel arch. The single framed nave roof is original but much restored. Instead of a tower there is a detached belfry which is a pyramidal roofed structure surrounded by a low stone-walled ambulatory. The font is 13th century and the north door and the fragments of old glass in the aisle west windows are 14th century. The pulpit, reader's desk, lectern, and communion rail are all Jacobean. On tomb chests are effigies of an early 14th century civilian and lady, and a later 14th century knight and lady. In the chancel are tablets to the wives of William and Essex Sherborne, d1660, and 1668, and there are larger tablets with pairs of putti to William Sherborne, d1671, and Thomas Trafford, d1685.

Pembridge Church   Ocle Pychard

Effigies in Pembridge Church

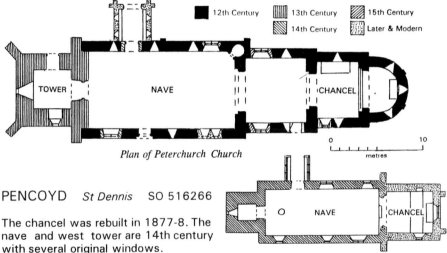

12th Century | **13th Century** | **15th Century** | **14th Century** | **Later & Modern**

TOWER | NAVE | CHANCEL

0   10

metres

Plan of Peterchurch Church

PENCOYD   *St Dennis*   SO 516266

The chancel was rebuilt in 1877-8. The nave and west tower are 14th century with several original windows.

NAVE | CHANCEL

Plan of Pencoyd Church

PETERCHURCH   *St Peter*   SO 345385

This large and little altered Norman church has four compartments, a nave, a former or intended central tower, a chancel, and an east apse. The south doorway, with an original door, and the arches between the compartments are decorated with chevrons. The apse has pilaster buttresses on the outside, and the tub-shaped font has rope mouldings and a nutmeg frieze. Later additions are the 13th century window in the chancel, a 14th century window in the nave, two 15th century windows in the central body, and the west tower begun c1280 and completed in the 14th century with a lofty recessed spire.

PETERSTOW   *St Peter*   SO 564249

The nave has one Norman north window and one 13th century lancet. The doorway, other windows, scissor-braced roof, and the chancel are 14th century. The thin west tower and spire are 15th century. The pulpit with blank arches is Jacobean.

PIPE-AND-LYDE   *St Peter*   SO 503441

George Kempson rebuilt the nave in 1874, leaving only the 13th century and Late Norman north and south doorways. He also added a broach spire to the 13th century west tower. The chancel is of c1300 and has a splendid roof with collars on arched braces with a trefoiled opening above. The rood beam with foliage also survives.

PIXLEY   *St Andrew*   SO 662388

The small single chamber has a tie-beam roof and old posts which now support a Victorian bell-turret. There are original lancets in the east wall and a later 13th century window, plus others of the 16th or 17th centuries in the south wall. The screen is old and the south doorway has a large 13th century hinge.

PRESTON-ON-WYE   *St Lawrence*   SO 384425

The church was heavily restored by T.Nicholson in 1883 but has a Late Norman doorway with chevrons on the arch and trumpet scallop capitals to the colonettes. Also Norman are one north window and the north doorway with a later head. The priest's doorway is of c1300 and the west tower and north transept are 14th century. The pulpit and the bench ends with leaf decoration are Jacobean.

PRESTON WYNNE   *Holy Trinity*   SO 558466

The church lies in a field. It was built in 1730 but the nave and chancel were both given new gothic features in the 19th century.

PUDLESTON   *St Peter*   SO 646376

The nave west wall has a Norman window looking into a tower of c1300 on which is a later medieval spire. The nave was rebuilt in 1813 and given aisles in 1851. The chancel is 13th century but has an east window and vestries of the 1850s.

Richard's Castle Church   *Pixley Church*

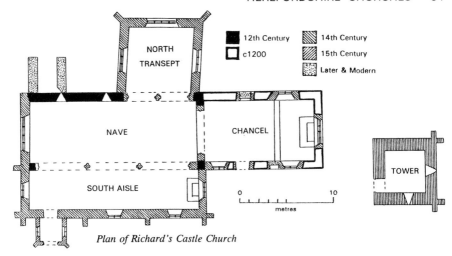

Plan of Richard's Castle Church

PUTLEY   *Dedication Unknown*   SO 646376

The nabve has two doorways and two windows of the 14th century. The chancel and long vestry are of 1875. The pulpit and screen contain reused Jacobean work. Much of the churchyard cross is preserved.

RICHARD'S CASTLE   *St Bartholomew*   SO 484703

This little-used church lies on a hill beside the castle. In order to help rather than hinder the defences it has a detached tower of c1300 to the east, overlooking the approach. The nave is Norman and has two original windows in the north wall. The chancel masonry is probably of c1190-1200, but the windows are 14th century, as are the south aisle with a three bay arcade, and the north transept with a two bay arcade. The pier of the latter and the chancel arch responds have castellated capitals with fleurons. The west window and porch are 15th century, and the unusual tracery of the transept end window may be 17th century. There was once a medieval vestry. Several windows contain fragments of old glass and there are box pews once dated 1688, and a 13th century coffin lid with a cross.

Grave-slab at Richard's Castle

Richard's Castle Church

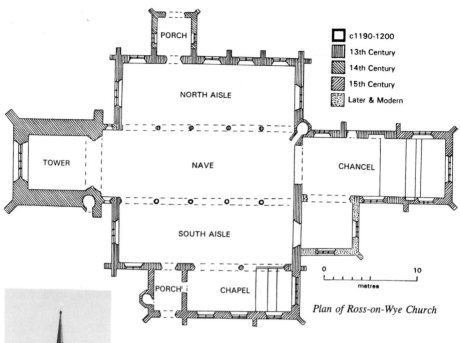

PORCH

c1190-1200

13th Century

14th Century

15th Century

Later & Modern

NORTH AISLE

TOWER

NAVE

CHANCEL

SOUTH AISLE

0   10

metres

PORCH   CHAPEL

Plan of Ross-on-Wye Church

Tower at Ross

ROSS-ON-WYE   *St Mary*   SO 598241

Ross has one of the largest churches in Herefordshire. The chancel and the wide aisles are of c1280-1300. The west tower and spire and the north porch are early 14th century. Later medieval additions are the east end of the chancel, the south porch, and the Markey chapel east of the latter. The south and north arcades are of c1200 and c1220-40 respectively. Their lower parts date from when they were raised in 1743. The font, pulpit and communion rail are all late 17th century. Four 15th century stained glass figures in the east window have come from the mansion of the bishops of Hereford at Stretton Sugwas. On an alabaster tomb chest are fine effigies of William Rudhall, d1530, Attorney General to Henry VIII, and his wife. There are tablets to William Rudhall, d1609, Nathaniel Hill, d1632, Elizabeth Markey, d1681, George Rudhall, d1729, a tomb chest with alabaster effigies of John Rudhall, d1636, and his wife, and a standing figure of William Rudhall, d1651.

ROTHERWAS   *Dedication Unknown*   SO 536384

The date 1589 on one of the tie-beams of the fine roof with queen-posts supporting hammerbeams with pendants refers to a rebuilding for Sir Robert Bodenham. One north window is 14th century, and others may be early 16th century. The west tower is probably 18th century. The east end is all Victorian.

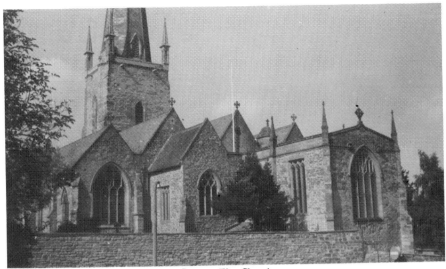

Ross-on-Wye Church

ROWLSTONE   *St Peter*   SO 374271

Both the nave and chancel have several original Norman windows and the south doorway has birds carved on the capitals of the shafts, a roll moulding, a band of rosettes, and a tympanum depicting Christ in Glory. There are also birds and figures on the capitals of the narrow chancel arch. The east window is 15th century, the tower is ancient but of uncertain date, and the south porch is Victorian.

ST DEVEREUX   *St Dubricius*   SO441312

The tomb recesses and paired lancets date the nave to the late 13th century, and the west tower may be of the same period. The chancel is late 14th century. There are ledgerstones to Thomas Goode, d1664, and Ann Goode, d1668, and fragments of several other 17th century monuments.

Plan of Rowlstone Church

0 [scale] 10
metres

■ 12th Century
▥ 13th Century
▨ 14th Century
▤ 16th Century
▦ 18th Century
▧ Later & Modern

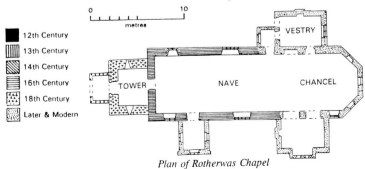

Plan of Rotherwas Chapel

St Margarets Church

ST MARGARETS   *St Margaret*   SO 354337

The narrow chancel arch, and probably the nave masonry, are Norman. One south window dates the chancel to c1300. Three domestic type windows may be 17th century and the porch may be 19th century. Much more important are the very finely carved rood screen and loft of c1520. The loft coving rests on two posts. See p17.

ST WEONARDS   *St Weonard*   SO 497243

The nave south wall and chancel arch are of c1300, and the chancel and south vestry are Victorian. The west tower and the north aisle and chapel are 16th century, although the arches of the four bay arcade to the aisle may be reused 13th century material. The porch is also 16th century and has a stoup with a large face. The chapel is closed off by original screens. There are fragments of old glass, a Jacobean pulpit, a 13th century dug-out chest, and an obelisk, urn, and cherub's heads in memory of Robert Minors Gouge, d1765.

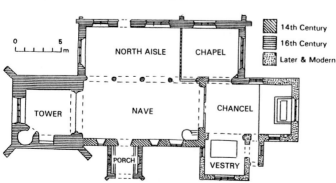

Plan of St Weonard's Church

Tower at Shobdon

Sarnesfield Church

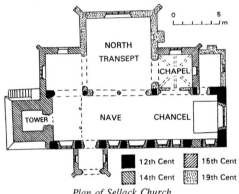

Plan of Sellack Church

St Weonards Church

SARNESFIELD   *St Mary*   SO 375510

The Norman nave has a west window looking into a tower of c1300 in which is reset another Norman window. The narrow south aisle with a four bay arcade is of c1190, but the doorway and two of the windows are of c1300. The chancel and south chapel, with a two bay arcade between them, are early 14th century. Also 14th century are the fine tie-beam roof over the nave, the timber south porch, and the stained glass figures in the south chapel. Outside, west of the porch, is the tomb of John Abel, designer of many fine timber buildings in Herefordshire, d1674, aged 97.

SELLACK   *St Tysilio*   SO 566277

The two eastern bays of a Norman three bay arcade and early 14th century aisle habe been obliterated by the erection of a Victorian north transept. Between the transept and the 19th century vestry is a vaulted 15th century chapel with a 13th century arch towards the 14th century chancel. Also 14th century are the south porch and the west tower with a broach spire. The pulpit and tester, the altar panelling, and the west gallery are Jacobean. The stained glass in the east window is of 1630 with older fragments. There are tablets to Helip Fox, d1768, William Powell, d1680, and Thomas Symonds, d1760.

SHOBDON *St John* SO 401628

Except for the 13th century west tower the whole church was rebuilt in 1752-6. It has a nave with shallow chancel bay screened off, and equally shallow transepts. The south transept accommodated the Bateman family who paid for the rebuilding, and the north transept seated their servants. The walls are ashlar faced externally with battlements and ogival Gothick arches. The interior is memorable, having a full set of contemporary matching furnishings painted white with light blue decoration.

On the hillside some distance north of the church and house is a folly formed from the re-erected chancel arch and doorways of the original Norman church of c1135, built to serve a small Augustinian priory later moved to Eye, and then to Wigmore. The doorway tympana represent the Harrowing of Hell and Christ in Glory, and the jambs have a profusion of dragons, birds, medallions, lions, interlace, chevrons, and human figures. The carvings are now very decayed but luckily drawings and reproductions survive of them before they crumbled away. See pages 17 & 84.

SOLLERS HOPE *St Michael* SO 613331

The nave, chancel and porch are 14th century. The windows are mostly 15th century with fragments of old glass. Two posts in the nave carry a timber belfry and spire. There is an incised slab of c1225 depicting a knight, and also a Jacobean pulpit.

STANFORD BISHOP *St James* SO 682516

The nave has two doorways, two windows and a font all of c1190. Another window of that period is reset in the 14th century chancel. The pryamidal-roofed west tower is early 13th century and there is a rebuilt 14th century porch. The south door is original, and there is a Jacobean pulpit and a medieval chair. There are several late 18th and 19th century tablets to the Freeman family of Stanford Court.

Stoke Edith Church

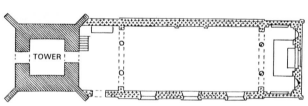

Plan of Stoke Edith Church

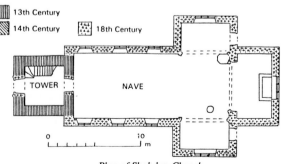

||||| 13th Century

     14th Century   18th Century

Plan of Shobdon Church

Folly at Shobdon of re-erected parts of Norman church   Stanford Bishop Church

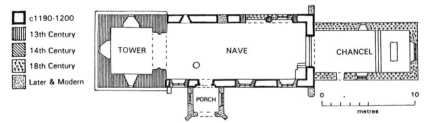

Plan of Staunton-on-Wye Church

STAUNTON-ON-WYE   St Mary   SO 376448

The nave of c1200 has round headed doorways and a small lancet, plus 14th century windows. The pyramidal-roofed west tower is of c1300 and contains 17th century panelling. Six medallions of c1540 fixed on the panelling were stolen in 1992. The 18th century chancel has Victorian windows. Only the crude two bay arcade remains of a former transeptal north chapel. Outside is a defaced 14th century female effigy.

STOKE EDITH   St Mary   SO 604407

The 14th century tower has a recessed needle-spire. The Foleys of Stoke Edith Park had the main body rebuilt in brick in 1740. It has five bays with big Tuscan columns dividing off the ends. Each end of the south wall has a doorway, but one is a dummy built for the sake of symmetry. Contemporary with the church are the font, pews communion rails, and three-decker pulpit. An alabaster effigy depicts a late 15th century lady with a butterfly head-dress. There is a large monument to Paul Foley, d1699, and two identical tablets to Henry Wolstenholme, d1738, and wife, d1749.

STOKE LACY   St Peter & St Paul   SO 621494

The rebuilding of 1863 by Kempson left only the Norman chancel arch and the low screen with a running leaf frieze on the cornice.

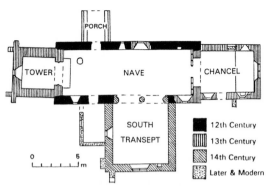

Plan of St Nicholas' Church, Sutton

12th Century

13th Century

14th Century

Later & Modern

Staunton-on-Wye Church

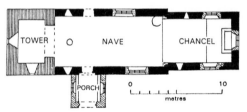

Plan of Stanford Bishop Church

STRETFORD   *St Peter*   SO 443558

In the 13th century the Norman church, of which one north window remains, was given a new chancel and a wide south aisle which now serves as the nave. The east and west windows are 14th century but the west wall itself is a Victorian rebuild. The original separate roofs were replaced c1530 by a new single span roof over the whole width. It has one tie-beam, arched braces to collar beams, and four tiers of cusped wind braces. The centrally placed belfry turret and the south porch may be of the same period. There is a Norman font and a Jacobean pulpit. The recess in the north wall has effigies of two couples of the Delabere family of c1320 and c1350.

STRETTON GRANDISON   *St Lawrence*   SO 633441

The roll-moulded priest's doorway is a reset piece of c1200. The nave, chancel, west tower and porch are otherwise all of c1300-50. A contemporary wall painting of a lady appears above the doorway. The Easter Sepulchre in the chancel has been cut through for access to a Victorian vestry. The font and pulpit are 15th century, and there is a tablet to Sir Edward Hopton, d1668, and his wife.

STRETTON SUGWAS   *St Mary Magdalene*   SO 460420

The new church of 1877-80 incorporates various relics of the old church. The timber framed upper parts of the tower and several of the windows are late medieval, there are old tiles in the vestry, one being dated 1456, and the tower doorway and south doorway tympanum carved with Samson and the Lion are Norman. An incised slab depicts Richard Grevelhey and his wife, d1473.

SUTTON   *St Nicholas*   SO 534454

The chancel and narrow nave are both of c1200, the chancel arch, north doorway, and two windows being of about that date. The west tower is 13th century, the south transept and its two bay arcade are early 14th century, and the chancel has three windows of c1300. The nave and chancel have 14th century piscinas with ballflowers. The timber north porch is 14th century. The screen has linenfold panels of c1520 in the dado, and there is a Jacobean pulpit.

SUTTON   *St Michael*   SO 527458

The small nave and chancel are both Norman and have three original windows. The four south windows are of c1300-20. In the west wall is the blocked arch of a former 13th century tower, now replaced by a timber porch. There is a Norman font with four busts of lions against the base and there is also a rare mid 17th century font in the form of a classical urn carried by a demi-figure of an angel holding a book. The tablet to Elizabeth Cotton, d1654, has standing allegorical figures, a pediment, puiit, and a corpse in a shroud.

TARRINGTON   *St Philip and St James*   SO 618408

Much of the church is Norman and there was originally an apse. The nave doorways with one order of shafts are original, that on the north being reset in the wall of the aisle added in 1835. Also Norman are two chancel windows, the chancel arch jambs, and the altered tower arch. The tower itself is 15th century and so are the large windows in the chancel. The nave south wall has been refaced. The font is late medieval and there are fragments of old glass. There is an old coffin lid with a cross and an effigy of a lady of c1340 set in a tomb recess of c1320 with ballflowers.

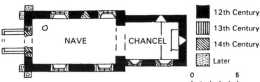

Plan of St Michael's Church, Sutton

Tarrington Church   *Tower at Stretton Sugwas*

TEDSTONE DELAMERE   *St James*   SO 696585

The church is reached by a path across a field with wide views to the east. The nave has two Norman windows of tufa and a 13th century lancet. The tiny chancel was rebuilt in 1856-7 by Sir George Gilbert Scott. The screen is late medieval, and there is a stand for an old hourglass in the porch. There are fonts of the 12th or 13th century and the 19th century lying beside each other.

TEDSTONE WAFRE   *St Mary*   SO 677591

Only a fragment of the south wall remains of the Earl Norman old church. The new church of 1873 designed by Haycock has been converted into a private residence.

THORNBURY   *St Anne*   SO 623597

The Norman nave has an original window beside a shafted doorway with chevrons on the arch. The massive west tower and the blocked three bay arcade of a former south aisle are 13th century and the nave has a north window of c1300. The chancel, vestry, and porch are of 1865 by Kempson. The Norman tub-shaped font has lozenges upon it.

THRUXTON   *St Bartholomew*   SO 437347

The west tower, the short chancel with a stained glass Crucifixion in a south window, the timber south porch, and the nave with its scissor-braced roof are all 14th century, the east window perhaps later than the rest. The font is dated 1677.

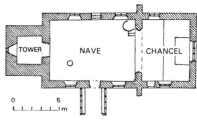

Plan of Thruxton Church

Tedstone Delamere Church

Thruxton Church

Thornbury Church

TURNASTONE *St Mary Magdalene* SO 357364

The Norman nave and the late 13th century chancel form a single undivided chamber. The nave has four late 13th century windows and the chancel east window is probably late 16th century. There is a fine ceiled roof with bosses and a simple Jacobean pulpit. There is an incised slab to Thomas Apparra, d1522, and his wife, and a tablet to Mrs Tranter, d1685, with rustic motifs and allegorical figurines.

TYBERTON *St Mary* SO 380399

Apart from the Late Norman south doorway, and the windows of 1879, this brick church and its furnishings are of 1719-21. There are monuments to William Brydges, d1668, Margaret Brydges, d1671, Anne Brydges, d1696, Francis Bridges, d1727, and his first wife, d1691, William Brydges, d1764, and Francis Brydges, d1793.

ULLINGSWICK *Dedication Unknown* SO 596500

The Norman nave has two original windows. It was lengthened to the west in the 13th century and a new chancel built c1300. The east window has a 15th century stained glass bust of the Virgin and Child. There is a recumbent effigy of John Hill, d1591, on a tomb chest, and a 13th century coffin lid with a floriated cross.

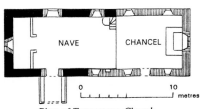

Plan of Turnastone Church

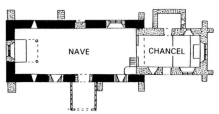

Plan of Tedstone Delamere Church

Upper Sapey Church

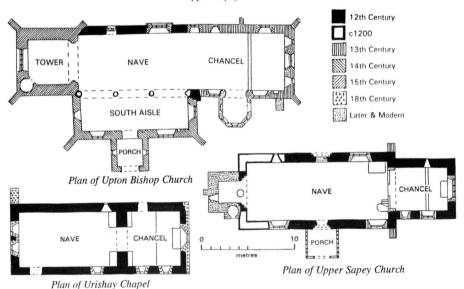

■ 12th Century

□ c1200

13th Century

14th Century

15th Century

18th Century

Later & Modern

Plan of Upton Bishop Church

Plan of Urishay Chapel

Plan of Upper Sapey Church

UPPER SAPEY   *St Michael*   SO 684637

The nave has two Norman doorways with two orders of shafts and chevrons on the arches, and the chancel has a Norman north window. The nave was lengthened westwards c1200 and has a window of that date. Two south windows are of c1300, and there are other windows, a chancel arch and a west tower of 1859, etc. The original Norman chancel arch, similar to the doorways, is reset as the new tower arch. Below it is a 13th century font. There are four plain early 16th century benches.

Arcade in Upton Bishop Church

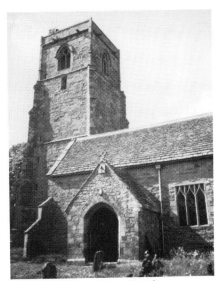

Upton Bishop Church

UPTON BISHOP   *St John the Baptist*   SO 651273

The nave has a blocked Norman north doorway. The three bay arcade is of c1180, but the aisle was rebuilt in the 14th century, and the porch then added. The 13th century chancel is the same width as the nave. It had three lancets in the east wall, but the middle one was replaced by a larger window in the 14th century. The west tower is of c1400, the font is 15th century, the pulpit is Jacobean, and there is a 14th century effigy of a civilian under an ogival canopy. On the chancel south wall is part of a Roman tombstone with a figure.

URISHAY   *Dedication Unknown*   SO 323376

Beside ruined Urishay Castle is a Norman chapel with a ruined nave and a recently re-roofed chancel the same width divided by a narrow round chancel arch. The doorways are old but the windows are 19th century.

Urishay Chapel

Walford-on-Wye Church

Plan of Walford-on-Wye Church

VOWCHURCH

St Bartholomew   SO 362365

One window, the font, and parts of the nave walls are Norman. The church was reconsecrated in 1348 after being extended into a long single chamber, now divided by a screen of 1613. Although it has some Jacobean decoration, the roof is 14th century work, as are the posts now supporting a bell turret of the 1520s. There are stalls with backs which are dated 1632 and a communion rail of the 1670s.

WACTON   SO 616574

Only footings remain of the church.

WALFORD-ON-WYE

St Michael   SO 587204

The church is mostly of various dates within the 13th century and comprises a nave with a north aisle with a four bay arcade, a chancel with an arcade of three small arches to a north chapel, and a north tower projecting beyond the chapel. The chancel south windows are 14th century and the east windows, north doorway, font and south porch are 15th century. The communion rail is of c1700, and there are tablets to William Adams, d1681, Edmund Yerne, d1707, John Stratford, d1738, and a group of other Stratfords up to 1709.

■	12th Cent
▥	13th Cent
▨	14th Cent
▧	15th Cent
☰	16th Cent
▨	17th Cent
▦	Later

0   10

metres

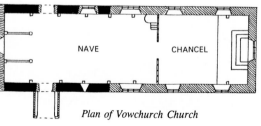

Vowchurch Church

Plan of Vowchurch Church

WALTERSTONE   *St Mary*   SO 340250

The Norman nave has a late medieval doorway and Victorian windows and bellcote. One of the two late 14th century chancel windows has 17th century glass. There are slate tablets to the Price family.

WELLINGTON   *St Margaret*   SO 497483

The spacious nave, the chancel arch, and the two doorways, one now reset in the aisle, are Norman. Of c1180-1200 is the massive west tower with pilaster buttresses pierced by windows. The chancel is late 13th century but the tomb recess within it is early 14th century, as is the south porch. Of the 15th century are the four bay arcade, the north aisle with its roof, and the north transept. The eastern end of the south side of the nave has been rebuilt. There is a tablet to Sir Herbert Perrot, d1683.

WELSH BICKNOR   *St Margaret*   SO 592177

A late 13th century female effigy lies in the church of 1857-9 beside the Wye.

WELSH NEWTON   *St Mary*   SO 499180

The church is mostly 13th century and forms a single chamber with a tiny west tower and spire flanked by lancets. It is covered by a wagon roof with ribs and bosses. The stone seat in the chancel may be 13th century. Of the 14th century are the very rare stone screen lighted by a dormer window and the porch. In the churchyard is the tomb of John Kemble, a catholic priest executed in August 1679. See p12.

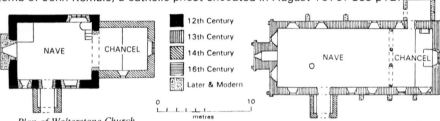

	12th Century
	13th Century
	14th Century
	16th Century
	Later & Modern

0   10
metres

Plan of Walterstone Church

Plan of Welsh Newton Church

Wellington Church

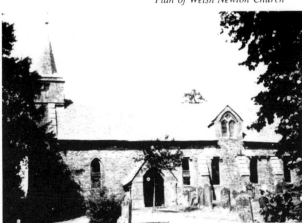

Welsh Newton Church

Weobley Church

WEOBLEY *St Peter and St Paul* SO 402519

The reset south doorway with chevrons is all that remains of the Norman church. The chancel and south aisle are late 13th century, and shortly before the consecration of three altars in 1325 a north transept and aisle and new five bay arcades were provided. Then the lofty NW tower with a spire connected to corner pinnacles by flying buttresses was begun. The chancel was lengthened in the late 14th century and the north aisle was widened in the 15th century.

Of the 14th century are the font and parts of a stone pulpit. In the north aisle are fragments of an old screen and five 15th century stained glass figures. In the south aisle is a 13th century coffin lid with a fine floriated cross in memory of Hugh Bissop of Norton Canon. The alabaster knight on a tomb chest may be William Devereux, d1430. There are alabaster effigies of Dame Alice Crutwell and John Marbury, d1437, and a statue of Colonel John Birch, d1691.

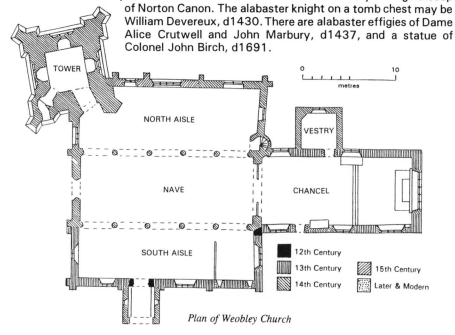

Plan of Weobley Church

Weston-Under-Penyard Church

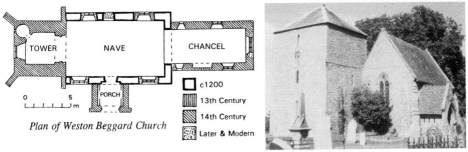

Plan of Weston Beggard Church

☐ c1200

▥ 13th Century

▨ 14th Century

▦ Later & Modern

Westhide Church

WESTHIDE   *St Bartholomew*   SO 586442

The pyramidal roofed tower is Late Norman. The wide south aisle with a two bay arcade and a recess with an effigy of a man holding his heart is 14th century. The tower west wall has been rebuilt. The nave north wall and chancel were renewed in 1866-7. An incised slab depicts Richard Monyington, d1524, and his wife and sixteen children, and there is a damaged Elizabethan slab with two figures.

WESTON BEGGARD   *St John the Baptist*   SO 584412

The doorways and chancel arch date the nave to c1200 although it was much rebuilt in 1881. The west tower, south porch, and chancel with two splendid tomb recesses are all of the 14th century.

WESTON-UNDER-PENYARD   *St Lawrence*   SO 632232

The nave and four bay north arcade are Late Norman. The aisle was rebuilt in the 14th century and a porch and west tower then added. The 13th century chancel has three east lancets. The nave has an old single-framed roof and there is a 17th century brass memorial.

Whitney Church

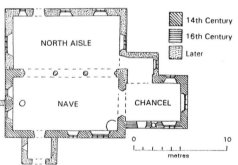

NORTH AISLE

14th Century

16th Century

Later

NAVE   CHANCEL

0   10

metres

Plan of Whitchurch Church

Whitbourne Church

WHITBOURNE   *St John the Baptist*   SO 725570

The nave south doorway with chevrons is Late Norman, and there is a Norman font with interlocked rosettes. The chancel and nave south wall are 13th century, the west tower and two south windows are 14th century, the chancel east wall is 15th century, and the aisle is of 1866. Inside is a tablet to Bellingham Freeman, d1689. Under the tower are many 18th and 19th century tablets to the Freemans of Gaines.

WHITCHURCH   *St Dubricius*   SO 557175

The nave and chancel with single framed roofs are 14th century. The south windows are later, the aisle is Victorian, and the font is Norman.

WHITNEY   *St Peter and St Paul*   SO 267475

The church was rebuilt in 1740 after a flood of the River Wye but older stones can be seen in the north wall of the nave and west tower. The pulpit and reredos incorporate Jacobean material. The west gallery must be of c1740. The panelling is older, and there is a door dated 1704, and a tablet to Thomas Williams, d1698.

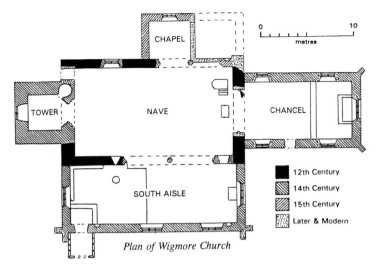

Plan of Wigmore Church

WIGMORE *St James* SO 413690

The wide Early Norman nave has herringbone masonry on the northern side and an original window, now internal, on the south. The west tower, the chancel, and the south aisle with a two bay arcade and its original roof with foiled wind-braces are 14th century, whilst the nave roof, with cusped wind braces, and the north chapel, of which only one bay now remains, are 15th century. The pulpit is early 16th century, and there are traceried old fronts to the stalls.

WILLERSLEY *St Mary Magdalene* SO 312474

This single chamber church now forms a private house. The Norman south doorway has rosettes, squares, and chevrons on the lintel. On the north side are a Norman window and a small 13th century lancet.

Wigmore Church

WINFORTON   *St Michael*   SO 298470

The timber framed upper stage of the pyramidal-roofed west tower is 16th century. The base may go back to the 13th century, the age of the nave south doorway. Two windows are of c1300, but most have been renewed. The pulpit is dated 1613 and the communion rail was given in 1701. The organ case is also early 18th century.

WITHINGTON   *St Peter*   SO 566435

The chancel, mostly rebuilt apart from one lancet, forms a single chamber with a nave with two Late Norman doorways. The west tower with a recessed spire is 14th century, two south doorways are 15th century. The screen with a cornice and cresting is of c1500.

WOLFERLOW   *St Andrew*   SO 668618

The church is mostly of 1863 and 1890-4 but the bell turret lies on old posts. The chancel arch, two doorways and much of the north wall are Norman. There is a late 13th century female effigy.

WOOLHOPE   *St George*   SO 612358

The chancel has one Norman window, perhaps reset, and there is a Norman two bay arcade. The aisle was widened and lengthened with a two bay arcade towards the chancel c1300. The west tower and the south aisle were also built c1300 but the aisle and its arcade are mostly renewed. In the north aisle are coffin lids of the 13th and 14th centuries with a lady in profile and crosses and foliage, and a 14th century effigy under a canopy with ballflowers.

WORMBRIDGE   *St Peter*   SO 427307

The nave has a north doorway of c1200 with several 13th century lancets, and the west tower is 13th century. The bell-stage, parts of the nave, and all of the chancel, date from the restoration of 1851-9. Under the tower and in the nave are portions of Jacobean woodwork brought here in 1870 from Newnham Paddox, near Lutterworth. There are fragments of 15th century glass in the chancel windows.

Woolhope Church   *Doorway, Wolferlow*

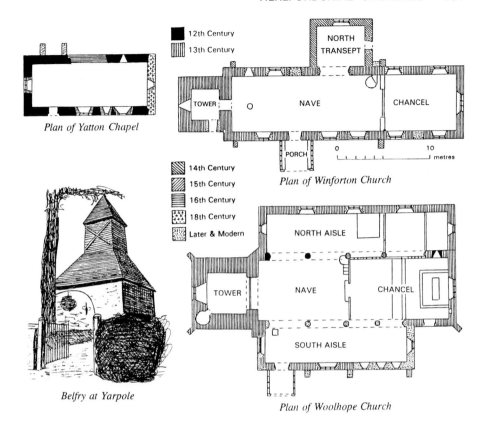

12th Century
13th Century
14th Century
15th Century
16th Century
18th Century
Later & Modern

Plan of Yatton Chapel

Plan of Winforton Church

Belfry at Yarpole

Plan of Woolhope Church

WORMSLEY   *St Mary*   SO 427478

This church is now cared for by the Redundant Churches Fund. It has a Norman nave with two original windows, a south doorway with an incised trellis and lozenges, and a 14th century north doorway and window. The chancel is 13th century, and there is a Jacobean pulpit. See page 102.

YARKHILL   *St John the Baptist*   SO 608427

The church was entirely rebuilt in 1862 except for the 13th century south doorway and the west tower, also 13th century, but with a Norman tower arch and a top of c1460. There are various old fonts.

YARPOLE   *St Leonard*   SO 470648

The nave and chancel were built c1300 but Scott rebuilt the latter in 1864 and added the north aisle. The nave roof with tie-beams and king-posts is original, and there is a 12th or 13th century font. The church's claim to architectural fame is the detached belfry to the south, probably of the 14th century, and having an original door. It is a wooden structure carried on four posts set within a stone outer wall. On top is a truncated pyramidal roof and spire.

Yatton Chapel

YATTON   *All Saints*   SO 627304

The old chapel by Chapel Farm is a humble single chamber, Norman in origin, with a doorway of that date, but with two 13th century windows, and rebuilding on the north and east sides in the 16th or 17th centuries and 1704 respectively. It is now disused. Probably from it are the posts and top rail of the screen in the new church of 1841 by William Roberts, which also has two 16th century foreign reliefs of Christ before Pilate and The Resurrection, and a lectern with late 17th century work.

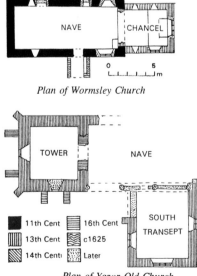

Plan of Wormsley Church

■ 11th Cent	☰ 16th Cent
▥ 13th Cent	▩ c1625
▧ 14th Cent	▨ Later

Plan of Yazor Old Church

Yazor Old Church

YAZOR   *St John the Baptist*   SO 404464

The ruins of the old church lie to the south of the new church of 1843 by George Rowe, to which the Price family monuments have been transferreed. The remains comprise a 15th century three bay arcade joining a 13th or 14th century west tower to a south transept of c1300 which occupied most of the south side, leaving space for an aisle only one bay long to the west.

OTHER ANGLICAN CHURCHES IN HEREFORDSHIRE

ADFORTON - St Andrew - 1875 by Seddon. Nave and apse.
BARTESTREE - St James - 1888 by Nicholson & Son. Nave, chancel & apse.
BISHOPSWOOD - All Saints - 1845 by John Plowman Junior.
BREDENBURY - St Andrew - 1877 by T.H.Wyatt. Pyramidal roofed tower.
FELTON - St Michael - 1853-4, spire added in 1891.
GANAREW - St Swithin - 1849-50 by John Pritchard. Nave and chancel.
HAMNISH CLIFFORD - St Dubricius - 1909-10 by W.J.Weatherley.
HARDWICK - Holy Trinity - 1851 in Decorated style.
HAREWOOD - St Denis - 1864. Disused single chamber.
HEREFORD - Holy Trinity - 1883 by F.R.Kempson, chancel 1907.
HEREFORD - St James - 1869 by Thomas Nicholson. Remodelled after fire 1902.
HEREFORD - St Martin - Entirely rebuilt 1845 by R.W.Jearrad. Chancel 1894.
HEREFORD - St Nicholas - 1842 by Thomas Duckham.
HEREFORD - St Paul - 1865 by F.R.Kempson. In Church Rd, Tupsley.
HOARWITHY - St Catherine - 1843, encased in 1885 by J.P.Seddon.
HOM GREEN (Ross on Wye) - Rebuilt by Bodley in 1905-6.
HUNTINGTON - St Mary Magdalene - 1850 by B. Cranstoun. Near Hereford.
LITTLE MARCLE - St Michael - 1870 by J,W.Hugall. Nave and chancel.
LONG GROVE - 1854-6 by Bodley. Nave and chancel.
MARSTON - 1855 by T.Nicholson. Nave and chancel.
MUCH BIRCH - St Mary & St Thomas of Canterbury - 1837 by Thomas Foster.
PENCOMBE - St John - 1864-5 by Thomas Nicholson. Nave, chancel and apse.
STAUNTON-ON-ARROW - St Peter - 1856 by Thomas Nicholson. Transepts & tower.
STORRIDGE - 1856 by Frederick Preedy. Nave, chancel & tower with broach spire.
TITLEY - St Peter - 1868 by E.Haycock Junior.
TRETIRE - St Mary - 1858 mostly. Nave and chancel.
WELLINGTON HEATH - Christchurch - 1840, rebuilt 1951.

FURTHER READING

A History of Herefordshire, John & Margaret West, 1985.
The Buildings of Herefordshire, Nikolaus Pevsner, 1963.
Transactions of the Woolhope Naturalists Field Club.
Royal Commission on Historical Monuments Inventories
    for Herefordshire, three vols 1932.
Hereford Archaeological News (published by the
    Woolhope Club Archaeological Research Section).

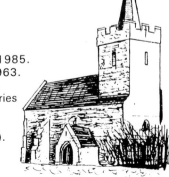

Dinmore Chapel

GLOSSARY OF ARCHITECTURAL TERMS

Abacus	- A flat slab on top of a capital.
Apse	- Semi-circular or polygonal east end of a church containing an altar.
Ashlar	- Masonry of blocks with even faces and square edges.
Baldacchino	- A canopy supported on columns.
Ballflower	- Globular flower of three petals enclosing a ball. Current c1310-40.
Baroque	- A whimsical and odd form of the Classical architectural style.
Beakhead	- Decorative motif of bird or beast heads, often biting a roll moulding.
Broaches	- Sloping half pyramids adapting an octagonal spire to a square tower.
Chancel	- The eastern part of a church used by the clergy.
Chevron Ornament	- A Norman ornament with continuous Vs forming a zig-zag.
Clerestory	- An upper storey pierced by windows lighting the floor below.
Collar Beam	- A tie-beam used higher up near the apex of the roof.
Corbel Table	- A row of corbels supporting the eaves of a roof.
Crossing Tower	- A tower built on four arches in the middle of a cruciform church.
Cruciform Church	- A cross-shaped church with transepts forming the arms of the cross.
Cusp	- A projecting point between the foils of a foiled Gothic arch.
Dado	- The decorative covering of the lower part of a wall or screen.
Decorated	- The architecture style in vogue in England c1300-1380.
Dog Tooth	- Four centered stars placed diagonally and raised pyramidally.
Easter Sepulchre	- A recess in a chancel which received an effigy of Christ at Easter.
Elizabethan	- Of the time of Queen Elizabeth I (1558-1603).
Fan Vault	- Vault with fan-like patterns. In fashion from c1440 to 1530.
Foil	- A lobe formed by the cusping of a circle or arch.
Four Centred Arch	- A low, flattish arch with each curve drawn from two compass points.
Hammerbeam Roof	- A roof carried on arched braces set on beams projecting from a wall.
Herringbone Masonry	- Courses of stones alternately sloping at 45 degrees to horizontal.
Hoodmould	- A projecting moulding above a lintel or arch to throw off water.
Jacobean	- Of the time of King James I (1603-25).
Jamb	- The side of a doorway, window, or other opening.
King-post	- An upright timber connecting a tie-beam or other opening.
Lancet	- A long and comparatively narrow window with a pointed head.
Light	- A compartment of a window.
Lintel	- A horizontal stone or beam spanning an opening.
Miserichord	- Bracket underneath hinged choir stall seat to support standing person.
Mullion	- A vertical member dividing the lights of a window.
Nave	- The part of a church in which the congregation sits or stands.
Nook-Shaft	- A shaft set in the angle of a pier or respond or jamb of a window.
Norman	- A division of English Romanesque architecture from 1066 to 1200.
Ogival Arch	- Arch of oriental origin with both convex and concave curves.
Pediment	- Low-pitch gable used in classical and neo-classical architecture.
Perpendicular	- The architectural style in vogue in England c1380-1540.
Pilaster	- Flat buttress or pier attached to a wall.
Piscina	- A stone basin used for rinsing out holy vessels after a mass.
Plinth	- The projecting base of a wall.
Quoins	- Dressed stones at the corners of a building.
Rere-Arch	- An arch on the inside face of a fice of a window embrasure or doorway.
Reredos	- Structure behind and above an altar forming a backdrop to it.
Respond	- A half pier or column bonded into a wall and carrying an arch.
Reticulation	- Tracery with a net-like appearence. Current c1330-70.
Rood Screen	- A screen with a crucifix mounted on it between a nave and chancel.
Sedilia	- Seats for clergy (usually three) in the south wall of a chancel.
Tester	- A sounding board above a 17th or 18th century pulpit.
Tie-Beam	- A beam connecting the slopes of a roof at or near its foot.
Tracery	- Intersecting ribwork in the upper part of a later Gothic window.
Transom	- A horizontal member dividing the lights of a window.
Triptych	- Three surfaces, usually sculpted or painted, joined by hinges.
Tympanum	- The space between the lintel of a doorway and the arch above it.
Victorian	- Of the time of Queen Victoria (1837-1901).
Wall Plate	- A timber laid longitudinally along the top of a wall.
Wind-Braces	- The struts used to strengthen the sloping sides of a gabled roof.